Schooling
for a fair go

Schooling for a fair go

Editors

John Smyth
Robert Hattam
Mike Lawson

The Federation Press
1998

Australia Foundation
for Culture & the Humanities

This project was supported by the Australia Foundation
for Culture & the Humanities and the Board of Research
of Flinders University. The Student Reference Group was
funded by the Australian Youth Foundation.

Published in 1998 in Sydney by
    The Federation Press
    71 John St, Leichhardt, NSW, 2040
    PO Box 45, Annandale, NSW, 2038
    Ph: (02) 9552 2200 Fax: (02) 9552 1681

National Library of Australia Cataloguing-in-Publication data:

    Includes index.
    ISBN 1 86287 296 1

    1. Education – Social aspects – Australia. 2. Education and state – Australia. 3. Public
    schools – Australia. I. Smyth, WJ (William John). II. Hattam, Robert. III. Lawson, Mike.

379.94

Typeset by The Federation Press, Leichhardt, NSW.
    Printed by Ligare Pty Ltd, Riverwood, NSW.

Preface

Australian have traditionally prided themselves on having one of the most egalitarian school systems in the world. In the post-war years it was not unreasonable to argue that schools were committed to educating for a fair go! Regardless of background, schools were seen as a social escalator for many. No longer. Today there is mounting evidence to suggest that this popular idiom is in deep and possibly terminal trouble, as user-pay reforms of the new "ruthless economy" drive deep wedges into an increasingly fragmented and deeply divided society. It seems that wealth, status and privilege are the central determining features of schooling for the new millennium. The various contributors to this book expose the erosion and corrosion occurring in public education, and provide an analysis of how the reclamation might occur through a restoration of schools as democratic public spheres. The kind of questions pursued are:

- what qualities of citizenship should Australian schools emphasise?
- what should be the focus of a distinctively Australian cultural studies in school curricula?
- how can education nurture a more democratic sphere?
- what is an appropriate educational response to the emerging forms of information technology?
- how can educators benchmark social objectives for education in a multi-cultural society, and how can we be sure we are achieving them?
- what should you look for in your neighbourhood school?

It is our sincere hope that this book will contribute in a small way to fostering the debate necessary for the resuscitation of public education.

John Smyth
Robert Hattam
Michael Lawson
September 1998

Contents

Acknowledgments

The editors want to thank the authors for their contributions and also acknowledge the support of Peter Botsman, Roy Martin, and Kym Davey for their thoughtful comments during the drafting process. Also to acknowledge Sarah Hattam, Roman Vaculik, Simon Maloney, Michelle Muldowney, Danielle Griffen, Megan Norris, Rebecca Taylor and Mark Purnell – members of the Student Reference Group.

List of Contributors

John Smyth – Professor of Teacher Education and Director of the Flinders Institute for the Study of Teaching, Flinders University of South Australia

Robert Hattam – Research Co-ordinator, Flinders Institute for the Study of Teaching, Flinders University of South Australia

Michael Lawson – Associate Professor and Deputy Director, Flinders Institute for the Study of Teaching, Flinders University of South Australia

James Ladwig – Senior Lecturer in the school of Education at University of Newcastle

Jennifer Gore – Senior Lecturer in the School of Education at University of Newcastle

Michael Garbutcheon-Singh – Associate Professor and Director of the Primary Teacher Education Program at University of Central Queensland

Bill Green – Professor of Cultural Studies at University of New England

Chris Bigum – Associate Professor in the School of Education at Central Queensland University

Geoffrey Shacklock was a Research Associate in the Flinders Institute for the Study of Teaching, Flinders University of South Australia

Michael Salvaris – Senior Research Fellow, Swinburne University of Technology

Lucas Walsh – Graduate Student, Swinburne University of Technology

1

Schooling for a fair go: (re)making the social fabric

Robert Hattam, John Smyth and Michael Lawson

Keeping alive an egalitarian sensibility

Most likely you will have left school (unless, of course, you teach in one) and will have picked up this book because the "fair go" part of the title sparked your interest. The title – *Schooling for a Fair Go* – aims unabashedly to locate our position and to raise, as a serious issue, the future of Australian schooling. It is our fear that Australian public schools are being taken in a direction that is the antithesis of an egalitarian sensibility – a sensibility that is against the intrusion of the market and is still alive and kicking in our public schools. We can be thankful that most of our public school teachers make decisions about their teaching practice using an ethical framework that has yet to be trampled by the logic of the market – a logic which privileges individualism over community, instrumental reason over ethics, and private ownership over common wealth. We also believe, perhaps naively, an egalitarian sensibility is still also highly regarded and alive and kicking in the Australian psyche or collective consciousness. We don't want to romanticise the past. There was no golden past in which Australia's schooling system did not favour the children of already wealthy families. For the rest – the large majority of Australians – it appears as though Tony Fitzgerald's conclusion to his report on *Poverty and Education in Australia* (1976) still rings true:

> that people who are poor and disadvantaged are victims of a societal confidence trick. They have been encouraged to believe that a major goal of schooling is to increase equality, while, in reality, schools reflect society's intention to maintain the present unequal distribution of status and power. (p 231)

Since writing this rather damning conclusion, teachers in public schools have continued to nurture a belief that schooling can make a difference. Many of Australia's teachers have worked in public schools to make the egalitarian myth a reality. As a consequence of this working against the grain of a powerful structural inequality that hides its face behind the rhetoric of choice, excellence and merit, a lot has been learned about how schools might work better for everybody's children and not just the privileged few. A trajectory based on a commitment for social justice and schools was developed during the 1970s through to the early 1990s. Largely worked out in schools, but supported by Federal and State governments, the idea of schooling for a fair go was given expression in a myriad of ways, including:

- reforms to the post-compulsory credentials that undermined the selecting and sorting function of schools and opened up curriculum options for a large group of students who had been denied meaningful and credentialled educational experiences;
- programs to improve the learning outcomes of girls, especially in areas of the curriculum that had been traditionally stereotyped as "boys only";
- the revamping of studies of Australian history that promulgated a racist history and simultaneously degraded Aboriginal culture;
- taking seriously the learning of languages other than English and the importance of nurturing these mother tongues for those children who have a non-English speaking background; and,
- developing inclusive approaches to teaching and learning based on collaboration, negotiation and assessment designed to give feedback on what has been achieved rather than odium for what has not.

Such an egalitarian sensibility understands that schooling is much more than just an opportunity for individuals to achieve a ticket into the labour market but also contributes to the social fabric of Australia.

To engage with this collection of essays we ask that you invoke both your memories of school as it was and your imagination for what it might be for future citizens of Australia. Just for a moment remember what your school was like. Try and remember the smells, the colours, the relationships, the teachers, the buildings, and your emotional reaction to all of these. What this collection of essays is about is imagining schooling, trying to make sense of where it has come from, what its present challenges are, and where it might go in the future.

Joining the din about what schools are up to

We hope that this book offers a space and a stimulus for joining in an important debate about how we organise formal learning for "our" children in schools. The school might be thought of as a technology for organising the teaching and learning that society designs for its children. Technology here is being given a broad definition and refers to a way of working the world. As educators, we want to join in the din being made about the design of that technology — about what our schools should be up to. All manner of interest groups, especially those from the business end of town, are making increasingly loud noises about what schools should be doing. That such conversations are often handled in spaces in which most of us are not welcome, is also part of our concern. We hope that this collection of essays can translate into a language accessible to a wider audience a set of important debates which are usually trapped in academic journals or in spaces designated for experts only.

This collection of essays raises questions about the school as a technology by focussing on some of the "big picture" issues in education — about the broad purposes of schooling in contemporary Australia and the complex relationship between schooling and culture. Trying to read the big picture is often seen as being unrealistic and utopian, or even indulgent. We believe that while some big picture stories are dangerous because they present a simplistic account, this is not always the case. Indeed, examination of the "grand design" for public education seems to be of particular importance at this time. Certainly those working to push the "free" market into all aspects of our lives are not afraid to think and act politically, using a big picture story about the advantages of market forces. The danger seems to lie not so much in developing a big picture as in applying that picture in a doctrinaire fashion without considering the potential effects of that application on all sections of the community — especially those who traditionally have been disenfranchised by societal arrangements. This moment in our history, in which the logic of the market in concert with the government is infecting our public institutions and civil society, is not the time to lose courage and retreat from a social analysis of schooling that uses big categories such as democracy, citizenship, culture and technology. The essays that follow have been written with that in mind.

Enacting the idea of schooling for a fair go, we believe, means making changes to schooling from the perspective of the least advantaged groups. From such a perspective, placing faith in the "private" sector and in the "free market" will result in unwanted outcomes for major sections of Australian society, particularly those who will be forced to rely on public institutions because they have no power in the market.[1] Simply put, the majority will become increasingly marginal. For these groups, the spaces for dialogue about their circumstances are presently being closed down. In the case of schooling, teachers and communities are being precluded from any real involvement in the development of educational policy. This has happened in the last two decades as governments and big business have combined to push on schools a narrow vocational purpose. Within the wider community the spaces for dialogue about working conditions also seem to have diminished during the 1980s and 1990s. It was in this context, across the transition from Keating's to Howard's Australia, that these essays were conceived.

Schooling culture and cultured schooling

To be interested in advancing schooling for a fair go in Australia requires exploring the relationships between schooling and culture in Australia. Culture in the broadest sense is a participatory activity, in which people create their societies and identities. "Culture lends significance to human experience by selecting from and organising it. It refers broadly to the forms through which people make sense of their lives" (Rosaldo 1989: 26). It is the contested ground within which we frame and interpret the events that involve us and others in society. Culture shapes individuals, drawing out and cultivating their potentialities and capacities for speech, action, and creativity. In turn the actions and creations of individuals and groups change the culture.

Australian culture then – understood to involve how we make sense of our lives – has a symbiotic relationship with schooling. Schooling is a significant site of social and cultural formation. Schools contribute to the nature of our culture because they assist in significant ways to the making of young identities. We learn about ourselves in our schools, as it is in school classrooms that we pass on what we consider to be our most important knowledge about the world and ourselves. Our schools are also sites of opportunity – places in which "our" children participate in a rite of passage into adult life and hopefully economic independence. Schools are places in which young people participate in the complex process of

---

1   England, New Zealand and the United States have all adopted a version of economic fundamentalism that has infected policies on schooling. See Ball et al 1996; Gordon 1994; Kelsey 1995; and Apple 1993.

4

"becoming somebody" (Wexler 1992). Of course, we are not asserting here that schools are the only influence – experiences of/in family, the media, the workplace, and for some, religion, are also important influences.

In schools then culture is written onto the consciousness of "our" children. The reverse is also true. What goes on in schools also works on culture. Not only are young minds worked on by culture through schooling but culture is worked on by young minds. Schools provide not only knowledge of the world but also resources to interpret and act on the world. From their schooling, young people act in and on the world and hence affect the culture they live in. Not only do young people contribute to the production of materials known as culture – music, art, dance, books – but they also contribute to an ongoing reformulation of the values and norms held by the population at large. That is, schools contribute to the nature of the social fabric of Australian society. The social fabric might be understood here to refer to the social and cultural capital that exists in society. Sociologists understand social capital to refer to:

> the actual or potential resources which are linked to possession of a durable network of more or less institutionalised relationships of mutual acquaintance and recognition. (Bourdieu 1986: 248)

and involve such phenomena as trust, reciprocity, mutuality (Cox 1995) participation in ceremonies and rituals (Luke 1993), solidarity, civic participation, and integrity (Putnam 1993). In the context of contemporary Australian society, then, schooling needs to be examined in terms of its contribution to (re)making the social fabric and hence contributing to Australia's pool of social capital.

Two interlocking questions emerge from these considerations:

1. What type of society do we want?
2. What will our schools have to be up to, to get the society we want?

In Keating's Australia

These essays were conceived out of, and in response to, the social milieu that was [Keating's] Australia. We bracket [Keating] as a means of indicating not only the man, Paul Keating, who stamped his own concerns on developing Australian society and culture through exercising power as the then prime minister, but also to indicate an ideology. Ideology here is given a generous spin and refers to an action-oriented set of beliefs. Even though it is fraught with difficulties because of the move away from traditional labour commitments, the [Keating] ideology might

5

be referred to as socially democratic – with a nasty streak of economic rationalism. Social democrats understand that racism, patriarchy and class distort the social arrangements and hence disenfranchise specific groups both in the exercise of power and in distributing shares of the national wealth. Social democrats, in their rejection of the simple logic of the "free" market, understand themselves as being much more than producers and consumers. They believe that the exercise of power in our democracy involves being able to manage difficult negotiations in ways that do not worsen the situation of less powerful groups in our society. As powerful examples: in [Keating's] Australia the difficult conversation was finally beginning with the Aboriginal population on resolving land rights issues in favour of some native title rights, issues for women were being given some prominence, and commitments to a universal health system, equity in education, the Human Rights Commission, and Legal Aid provisions were being maintained, though there were signs that some of these commitments were coming under threat.

During the development of [Keating's] corporate federalism the single biggest threat to public education came from the marketising agenda of various State governments. This meant that schools were being pushed through a process of devolution, involving a shift of responsibility from government to community in which the schools were encouraged to reconstruct themselves as "self-managing". In some cases the result might more aptly be termed "the self-damaging school". Devolution often meant that school communities were asked to take on a set of responsi-bilities that were once assumed by government, without a commensurate transfer of resources or power. School principals found themselves having to make decisions about where to make the cuts due to shrinking budgets, or how to make teachers work harder with fewer resources, or how to follow a new set of curriculum directives. The devolution of power from centre to periphery has, to a large extent, been illusory. Public education is still on a tight rein.

At the same time schools were facing pressure to take on an extra set of social issues. During the last months of the Keating regime the focus on a possible change in the structure of the future Australian nation from monarchy to republic was associated with issues such as how to enact principles of participatory democracy in schools, citizenship education, the growth of information technology in schools, and how schools might respond to the call for cultural understanding. Thus, while public schools were facing increased pressure to respond to calls for increasing productivity, greater accountability, and higher levels of fundraising, they were also being called upon to participate in the reshaping of major parts of the social fabric.

Howard's world

With the arrival of [Howard] – and his neo-liberal ideology – both sets of pressures have increased, though not necessarily because the same messages are being fed to the public education system. In some areas of social action, especially the move to republican status, the establishment of appropriate relationships with indigenous people and the maintaining of an adequate social welfare safety-net, the [Howard] regime has retreated from previous Commonwealth commitments. The urge to privatise public resources has been difficult to resist and the expenditure of government resources on public services seems increasingly a matter of dispute. Although the rate of collection of contributions from citizens through taxation has been maintained, it seems that it is simple-minded to expect that these resources should be used to support public activity.

In this uncertain climate, schools are under pressure to demonstrate achievement of a new set of social and economic objectives. The uncertainty is increased by the fact that the objectives are diverse, even contradictory. Schools are expected to educate in order to maximise the potential of the individual, and yet are also expected to be able to deliver jobs by directing students into specific vocational channels. This has been the response of governments to those in business who have been calling upon schools to adopt vocational preparation as their major objective. Direct vocational training is once again being seen as a way for schools to contribute to the solution of youth unemployment. Indeed, in contemporary Australia the school is being seen as the proper place for the young, for at least the first two decades of their lives. Governments are becoming more transparent in their use of the education system to assuage the problems of youth unemployment, and in some of the most recent Federal government thinking there is a deliberate desire to have all young people in school until at least the age of 18 years, and preferably in some form of "edutraining" for several years beyond that age.

Those working in schools are also affected by the cultural shift that has occurred in Australia under [Howard's] ideology. Schools by their very nature have to come to terms with how a society manages the difficult negotiations around recognising the "identities of cultural and disadvantaged minorities" (Gutman 1994: 3). Under [Howard], important recent reforms to schooling are now under attack on the grounds of political correctness, black arm-band history, and the use of non-sexist language, to name but a few.

Re-imagining schools

The chapters in this book raise a number of issues that are crucial to sustaining and maintaining a vibrant public democratic sphere, and the role of schooling in doing that. All of the chapters are concerned in one way or another with making the case for what it might mean to re-vision and re-imagine schools as the centrepiece through which this democratic restoration can occur. In different ways each of the authors makes the claim that democratic forms of schooling are the way to move beyond the decline of public institutions, the current sense of crisis and paralysis, and widespread youth pessimism, and to respond to the cries for a reappropriation of technical, human, cultural and social capital.

"It is not easy being an Australian"

In arguing that "It is not easy being an Australian", Garbutcheon-Singh claims that the school curriculum needs to be reinvented for dramatically changed times. In particular, he sees this happening in four ways: (i) establishing a broad set of socially critical benchmarks that provide a focus on issues of cultural distinctiveness, minority stereotyping, institutionalised discrimination, targeted government cutbacks, and the absence of leadership that creates an intellectual and moral vacuum about the root causes of poverty and unemployment; (ii) a politics of difference that provides voice for indigenous and ethnic minorities, and the wider sociocultural conditions for freedom, and where there is a genuine commitment to eliminating disadvantage and alleviating vulnerability; (iii) the translation of these wider ideals into a set of social objectives for education based on classroom and curriculum practices of inclusivity, the challenging of cultural imperialism, and the use of the best features of ethnic minorities for culturally responsive education; and (iv) achieving these social objectives for education through dialogic forms of education that examine the strengths and weaknesses of Australian society, examining silences and instances of sexism and racism, while building cross-sectoral support for the marginalised on the basis of citizen action competencies.

"Retooling schooling"

Bigum and Green describe a different kind of educational response – this time to the new digital technologies – but one that is still largely driven out of school engagement with consumption, image and impression management, rather than the need to create an informed, participatory citizenry. The overwhelming presence of the market takes expression on this occasion through a high tech imperative of schools to compete with one another for students, and to use sophistication in educational technology as the instrument with which to do this. The argument bears similarities to that of Garbutcheon-Singh in that curriculum still has to be re-invented – this time in terms of the distinctive image and way of "doing education" or "making it happen". Bigum and Green's claim is that there is a lack of an appealing social and educational vision for the young; that we need to understand how schooling is a distinctive form of educational technology, and how information technology has the capacity for re-tooling society in a context of crisis. Rather than schooling being "spaces of enclosure", we need to see it instead, they argue, as opportunities for new forms of "openness" through flexible delivery, new forms of distributive learning, and different arrangements of sites, bodies and technologies. The basis for this re-tooling needs to be a commitment to education as a critical democratic practice that focusses less on technology per se and more on the social purpose that information technology permits. Developing and cultivating "informed scepticism" so as to move beyond limited rehearsals currently experienced will necessitate an "educationally principled approach, reflecting social justice", and where teachers are supported first. This "teachers first" approach acknowledges the technical disadvantage of many teachers and a "pronounced professional insecurity". Issues of information technology need to be seen in cultural-critical terms, rather than simply technical ones; technocultural capital, who gets it, and who is disadvantaged by it ought to be prominent school agenda.

"Doing critical cultural studies in schools"

Hattam, Shacklock and Smyth argue that a distinctively critical Australian cultural studies will only emerge when the range of possibilities are opened up by including the practical affairs of everyday life – the media, fashion, sport, entertainment, cinema, lifestyle images – in the body of texts to be unmasked in a study of culture. Enabling youth to resist other people's positioning of the texts of mainstream and practical culture, will provide youth with the kind of multiliteracies and the democratic space from which to speak. Adopting the kind of "democratic imaginary" that provides youth with a capacity to understand the context of their lives, is in marked contradistinction to that created for them by the corporate ideological system of the media, and is much more anchored in the aspirations, generative themes and lived experiences of youth.

At the level of schools and classrooms, all authors endorse some form of "dialogical pedagogy" (Fernandez-Balboa and Marshall 1994) where the explicit intention is to "read the word and the world", which is another way of saying: to look at the world in interdisciplinary ways, drawing on a range of theoretical perspectives, and interrogating everyday experiences, practices, histories, cultures and traditions. Searching for distinctiveness within and while developing educational and cultural diversity, is seen as residing in forms of pedagogy that pursue questions like:

Why are things the way they are?

How did they get to be this way?

What sets of conditions/relationships support the dominant forms of daily life?

What then is to be done?

Developing an active from of citizenship

The qualities of citizenship are increasingly being defined, Walsh and Salvaris argue, within a narrow "user pays" discourse of economic rationalism. Broad processes of social and civic participation and devotion to the common good are being usurped and replaced by increasingly narrow legal definitions of citizenship, and emasculated by limited notions of "choice". Active participation in the political life of the nation is being expunged by regulated exchange between client and state. While there are clear limits to what education can do in this situation, Walsh and Salvaris claim that schools nevertheless do still have considerable scope for manoeuvre in how they pursue democratic principles. Schooling can encourage domestication, for instance, through competitive assessment and didactic teaching. Utterances about tolerance, multiculturalism and equality, can sound very hollow within authoritarian structures. And the social organisation of schools can reinforce patterns of social domination through "visible staff hierarchies". Participatory pedagogies of various types, along with a high degree of student involvement relevant to their own experiences and lives, is conducive of classrooms where being a "good citizen" is more than tokenism. Incubating democratic citizenship in classrooms and having schools that model active democratic citizenship are argued to be part of the process of transcending the limits of schools as state controlled and regulated institutions, thereby producing future citizens capable of taking a wider responsibility in the public interest.

If education for citizenship is to be effective it seems reasonable to argue that such education should be grounded in the students' experiences in the school. If citizenship is to be characterised by active participation then the student needs to be able to identify the central features of such activity and so needs to have experienced active involvement in decision-making. A similar case can be made for experience in critical action, action that promotes understanding of the genesis and underpinnings of the institution. In an era when critical literacy is embedded in school language programs it is hardly radical to argue the necessity for students to adopt similar perspectives with regard to their social and political experiences at school. Indeed we have seen effective examples of participation, in politically literate ways, in junior primary schools in the struggling communities of northern Adelaide. These schools have shown that it is possible to engage students in a politically literate way in their schools, while developing among students a sense of their civic duties.

Schooling for a more democratic public sphere

Gore and Ladwig argue for a platform from which to nurture a more democratic public sphere in which critical and political literacies are fundamental rather than an add-on. While they list some notable successes in Australian schools (the Disadvantaged Schools Program, special education, rural and remote education, girls education, Aboriginal and non-English speaking background education), the groups for whom these programs were developed still suffer from institutionalised disadvantage, often exacerbated by school practices such as student labelling, ability grouping, accelerated learning, behaviour management policies, and the systematic exclusion of multiple curriculum voices/experiences. The kind of reforms argued to be necessary for democratic education are ones that emphasise active participation, where students are critical about their learning, and in which schools are organised so they sustain a pedagogy that produces equitable learning outcomes. The challenge is not so much in knowing what to do, but rather in how to sustain it over periods of time for all students. Being vigilant about the politics of exclusion and resentment, in these situations, means pursuing policies, practices and reforms that "most advantage the least advantaged".

As sites of cultural formation, schools are crucial in the formation of democracy. In contemporary classrooms students are already actively managing their cognitive and social lives. They are making decisions about what they will attend to and how seriously they will treat that material. The more critical they are in this management the more likely it is that they will develop deeper understanding of the material they are studying. This is the view of learners that is espoused during teacher training and it is also the view of learning that school systems include in mission statements and statements of priorities. Within this perspective teachers are encouraged to engage students directly in investigating the nature of learning and to call upon students to accept the responsibilities they have as self-regulating learners.

How well does the official rhetoric match the practice? We can ask this question about both classrooms and schools. In each situation, is the learner encouraged to participate fully in relevant decision-making? Is the student in the classroom encouraged to develop the capacity to manage study tasks effectively? At the school level, to what extent are students encouraged to manage their activity in institutional decision-making? The two spheres of action for students, those of learning and of the school as community, could be organised so that their principles of organisation and practice become complementary. It would also be easy to keep these spheres of action separate so that students could be expected to be active in one but not in the other. Yet, as argued above in the case of the citizen and the state, it seems unlikely that the student will maximise active involvement in learning in a classroom if the immediate context in a school rejects a similar type of involvement in institutional decision-making.

One final issue is stimulated by the discussion of democracy here. This is concerned with the role of the public institution in the maintenance of our democracy. In several chapters we are reminded of the symbiotic relationship between state and citizen. As noted earlier, our democracy assumes that both state and citizen share the responsibility for the operation of this system of governance. Both have rights and duties. The question to be raised in the current economic and political climate focusses on the extent to which the state is fulfilling its responsibilities to the citizen. Through the privatising of some social services, or through the establishment of these on a market basis, the state can be seen to be shirking its responsibilities to sections of its citizenry. This shirking of responsibility occurs because the transfer from public to private sphere can act to exclude sections of the community from such services in a way that compromises the democracy.

Such compromise is also possible through inactivity on the part of the state. The manifestation of inactivity that we draw attention to is the current widespread practice of collapsing the sphere of public activity by privatising or marketising activities that have traditionally been the province of the state. Privatising and marketising of public functions and institutions is justified almost solely on economic grounds, so that the citizen-as-consumer is argued to be advantaged by the predicted availability of cheaper products and services. Usually absent from such accounting calculations is the estimation of social costs. In the private sector in Australia the recent debates about the role of tariffs provides a clear example of the social costs that are to be offset against the advantage of lower prices. While the latter effect on price is easily quantified, the difficulty of estimating the costs associated with the consequential social effects means that such effects are often ignored.

There is an urgent need to examine how to re-establish reciprocity in relationships between the citizen and the state in circumstances where the market is beginning to completely prevail and where being a citizen is rapidly becoming conflated with being a consumer. The recognition that a diminution in the responsibility of the state produces a concomitant reduction in group and civic duty is a necessary precursor to the recuperation of the contemporary relationship between the citizen and the state. Being a citizen, therefore, brings with it a set of collective responsibilities, but these need to be matched by a concern and compassion by the state for the wider collective collectivity – a notion that is rapidly being depleted as a consequence of the marketisation of society.

The chapters in this book draw attention to the intimate relationships between the school, culture and democratic forms of government. There are interesting parallels between the characteristic features of democratic schools and of a democratic society. Schools can provide the type of education required for the development of effective citizens. For this to occur it seems clear that the operation of the school both within the classroom and outside it must model democratic principles. The greater challenge is to ensure that the wider culture and our public institutions support, rather than undermine, the cultural formation of the young being enacted in the nation's schools.

References

Apple, M. (1993) *Official Knowledge: Democratic Education in a Conservative Age*. New York: Routledge.

Ball, S., R. Bowe et al (1996) "School Choice, Social Class and Distinction: The Realization of Social Advantage in Education". *Journal of Education Policy*, 11(1), 89-112.

Bourdieu, P. (1986) "The Forms of Capital" in J. Richardson (ed) *Handbook of Theory and Research in the Sociology of Education*. New York: Greenwood Press.

Cox, E. (1995) *A Truly Civil Society – 1995 Boyer Lectures*. Sydney: Australian Broadcasting Corporation

Fernandez-Balboa, J. and J. Marshall (1994) "Dialogical Pedagogy in Teacher Education: Towards an Education for Democracy". *Journal of Teacher Education*, 45(3), 172-182.

Gordon, L. (1994) "'Rich' and 'Poor' Schools in Aotearoa". *New Zealand Journal of Educational Studies*, 29(2), 113-125.

Gutman, A. (1994) Introduction in C. Taylor (ed) *Multiculturalism: Examining the Politics of Recognition*. Princeton (NJ): Princeton University Press.

Kelsey, J. (1995) *Economic Fundamentalism: New Zealand Experiment – A World Model for Structural Adjustment*. London: Pluto Press.

Luke, A. (1993) "Genres of Power? Literacy and the Production of Capital" in R. Hasan and G. Williams (eds), *Literacy in Society*. London: Longman.

Putnam, R. (1993) "The Prosperous Community: Social Capital and Public Life". *The American Prospect*, 13 Spring, 35-42.

Rosaldo, R. (1989) *Culture and Truth: The Remaking of Social Analysis*. London: Routledge.

Wexler, P. (1992) *Becoming Somebody: Towards a Social Psychology of the School*. London: Falmer.

2

Nurturing democracy in schools

James Ladwig and Jennifer Gore

A society which makes provision for participation in its good of all its members on equal terms and which secures flexible readjustment of its institutions through interaction of the different forms of associated life is in so far democratic. Such a society must have a type of education which gives individuals a personal interest in social relationships and control, and the habits of mind which secure social changes without introducing disorder. (John Dewey 1916: 99)

Throughout most of the 20th century, philosophers have readily acknowledged that an education which truly promotes democracy is far more than the conventional ideas and practices found in modern schools. While schooling has been seen as central to the development of any form of society, of any polity, a democratic society requires specific forms of schooling. As the words of Dewey remind us, that form of schooling is fundamentally linked to specific cultural values and habits of mind, with concrete and unswaying commitments to create a public, social life. Thus, when Australians ask what an Australian democratic society and culture would look like, the fundamental links between that culture, schooling and democracy need to be firmly addressed. To the extent that this essay may help stimulate debate, we hope that its audience does not lose sight of the fact that such a debate is precisely about naming just what form of "public" Australia should be.

How can education nurture a more democratic public sphere?

Democracy is fundamentally about the active participation of a society's citizens in making decisions about the functioning of that society. If education is to nurture a more democratic society, then schools must provide for all citizens a minimal essential education. This provision is necessary not only for a society's children, but also for its adults. For instance, in a complex society such as Australia, which still suffers from

15

significant levels of basic adult illiteracy, the same level of minimal essential education made available to children in schools should be provided for adults. But what is this minimal essential education?

Most people would accept that a minimal essential education for all includes a set of basic technical, scientific, historical, and cultural literacies (or competencies). Of course, there are debates over specific competencies and over what constitutes a minimal level of education. In general, however, there is wide agreement that people need to be able to read and write, to understand basic scientific method, to appreciate aspects of the historical development of the globe and nation, and to develop some cultural capital and skills. We would argue that a minimal essential education also includes a set of critical social and political literacies that enable the analysis of public debates and institutions. As Amy Gutman (1987) puts it:

> Children must learn not to just behave in accordance with authority but to think critically about authority if they are to live up to the democratic ideal of sharing political sovereignty as citizens. (p 51)

Indeed, to the extent that democracy functions on the basis of a set of moral principles including justice and liberty, what we are calling critical literacy must be seen as fundamental rather than as an accessory to basic education.

One of the stated goals of the Federal Government for Australian school education is the increased retention of students to Year 12. Such a goal would appear realistic given the sharp increase in retention rates during the past two decades (Johnston 1990). If schools participate in the shaping of young people's lives for a full 12 years or more, and hence in the shaping of society, we must seriously examine the opportunities and responsibilities that confront education. It no longer makes theoretical sense, for instance, to speak of "primary" and "secondary" education (Gutman 1987). We would argue that basic and critical literacies necessary for full participation in society cannot be accomplished without high school education. In the contemporary context of high technology, dense media filtering, and complex economies, the *minimal* essential basic and critical literacies necessary to prepare students for their citizenship role in democratic society require the sustained educational interaction that full retention would enable.

Questions emerge, however, about the extent to which schools equip students with these literacies. When we consider popular debates surrounding the last Federal election, for example, it is clear that many people (including many young people) lack sufficient understanding of party political processes to really make the informed choice that is their democratic right and, in this country, their democratic responsibility. Even at the level of basic literacy in language and numeracy, we know that schools have not been able to provide for all people despite substantial rhetorical and actual commitment to such educational outcomes. In order to move toward a fuller examination of the role of education in nurturing a more democratic public sphere, we must first consider what we know about schools' failure to provide a minimal essential education for all.

At the "broad" level of schools and school systems, policy makers and bureaucrats are constantly confronted with questions about how resources and educational outcomes are to be distributed across populations. Policy rhetoric in Australian education has moved from an "equal opportunity" to an "equal outcomes" commitment, acknowledging that schools must do more than set up opportunities for students to choose particular learning experiences or subject pathways if levels of attainment are to improve for historically disadvantaged groups. While we fully support this shift in commitment, such traditional measures of "opportunity" as participation and attendance rates ought to be acknowledged in the assessment of schools' accomplishments in providing quality education for all. In a context of limited economic and personnel resources, gains in such measures, especially for groups who have previously been under-represented, are indicative of greater provision for all. On the other hand, however, in this context of limited resources, decisions are made about what constitutes an adequate education for particular groups of students and this level often falls far short of the basic let alone critical literacies that we have argued are essential for democratic participation.

When it comes to attainment or achievement, these inadequacies of schooling are starkly evident, particularly as they are differentially manifested according to social group (Teese 1995). A recent statement from the New South Wales Director-General of School Education, Dr Ken Boston, provides a working definition of educational equity:

> If we are genuine in seeking real equity, then our goal must be for the educational performance of any one group of students to approach that of the student cohort of which they are a part (*School Education News*, 20 July 1994).

That is, we must seek performance outcomes for any specific group of students (such as girls, or students of non-English speaking background) which are equivalent to those of the entire student population enrolled in the same year. As this definition highlights, equity is a social issue and not necessarily an individual one.

We know that school works better for some groups of students than for others. Australia has done better than many other countries in developing programs and policies designed to achieve greater equity. The Disadvantaged Schools Program, designed to support schools with clientele from poor socioeconomic backgrounds, is one such example. Resources have also been directed towards special education, students from rural and remote areas, girls' education, the education of Aboriginal and Torres Strait Islander students, as well as students from non-English speaking backgrounds. If education is to nurture a democratic public sphere, by providing a minimal essential education for all, such equity programs must be maintained and expanded.

We also know that despite these programs, and despite their positive effects for the groups they have targeted, the same groups remain disadvantaged. Even in the case of gender equity, where school outcomes are (arguably) more equal than previously, girls remain disadvantaged in terms of post-school options and pathways. Hence, while equity programs are necessary for producing the democratic outcomes fundamental to a truly democratic society, they are insufficient.

For instance, we know that a number of systemic school practices are related to the production of educational inequalities. One set of practices relates to differences between schools and school systems. With increases in the development of specialist schools, public funding for private schooling, and in processes of parent/school choice, the provision of quality education for all potentially is undermined. for instance, private schooling is inherently premised on notions of hierarchical provision of education rather than universal provision, on the idea that some students should receive a different (and by implication, better) quality of schooling.

A second set of practices that contributes to the production of educational inequality relate to internal school/curriculum organisational differences. For instance, we know that streaming and tracking[2] (both formal and informal) contribute to greater inequality. We also know that such systemically promoted classroom practices as student labelling,

---

2 Tracking and streaming are terms used to describe various schooling practices which sort students into relatively fixed groups for instructional purposes according to perceived shared characteristics such as "ability", for long periods of time.

ability grouping, ill-informed adaptations of "multiple intelligence" theories, lack and misuse of cooperative learning, and so-called "accelerated learning", are of dubious value (and often of documented harm) when it comes to promoting equality of outcomes.

Schooling has always functioned in complex ways in relation to democracy. Historically, mass public schooling developed with strong regulatory functions and purposes. That is, schools were established for the control of populations, and have broad disciplining effects (both good and ill). Within the classroom, for instance, where the balance between "classroom management" and "teaching" is a consistent concern of teachers, there is necessarily a complex functioning of power relations which sanctions teacher authority for democratic outcomes. The inconsistencies of requiring students to sit, by compulsion not choice, in classrooms in which they have little input or control, while we attempt to teach them to think for themselves and to participate in decision-making are clearly evident. Bernstein (1990) has argued that pedagogy[3] is more than a relay for power relations external to itself. Indeed, pedagogy has its own power relations which can easily undo democratic social and political agendas (Gore 1995).

In addition to the pedagogical process itself, concerned educators have described both curricular and instructional practices that have excluded multiple voices/experiences within classrooms. There is a long-standing literature within the sociology of education that has elaborated the way in which schools connect best with, and work best for, students of middle class, Anglo, male backgrounds.

What reforms to all schooling are seen as essential for democratic education?

> [A] democratic public should provide mechanisms for the effective recognition and representation of the distinct voices and perspectives of those of its constituent groups that are oppressed or disadvantaged. (Young 1990: 184)

Clearly we know a great deal about the ways in which schools have not provided equitable outcomes, and we also know a fair amount about educational programs that have been developed to deal with specific

---

3   We use the term *pedagogy* here, rather than *teaching*, to emphasise not only how one teaches but also what is being taught, how one learns and the contexts in which knowledge (both formal and informal) is produced.

groups of people who have not traditionally received an equitable education through schooling. However, this leaves open the question: What kind of schooling works for the overall population to produce an equitable democratic education?

The very idea that certain sets of skills, forms of knowledge and dispositions are needed for anyone to participate in a democratic society implies that those skills, forms of knowledge and dispositions need to be developed in students. After all, if a democracy requires its citizens to be able to actively join in a collective decision-making process, each new generation of future citizens needs to develop the knowledge, skills and dispositions required by that democracy.

This obviously poses a challenge for educators to develop and employ forms of pedagogy and curriculum that emphasise active, participatory learning, and to organise schools in a way that sustains these forms of pedagogy. This is not a new issue for educators, who have long been concerned with the promotion of democratic forms of teaching, and the basic outlines of ways in which students can participate more fully in their own learning are relatively easily found in educational literature.

Roughly speaking, while there are disagreements on details, there is remarkable agreement among educators that active student participation in their own learning is valuable. That is, students' active participation in their own learning has been promoted by psychologists for cognitive and moral development, by philosophers and sociologists for moral and political reasons, as well as by more economically minded educational reformers for reasons of efficiency and productivity. While there is debate about how to balance the degree to which teachers and students provide direction and input in democratic forms of pedagogy and curriculum, there is a broadly shared commitment among democratic educators to students having a say in guiding their own learning.

While it is possible to at least imagine some consensus on the value of democratic pedagogy and curriculum (although that certainly is not a foregone conclusion), it is much more difficult to imagine how schools might be organised to sustain democratic learning. It is not as though we have no ideas on which to base attempts to restructure schooling to promote democratic pedagogy and curriculum, however; the history of educational reform includes many powerful examples of more radical school structures designed specifically to promote active student participation. From "open schools" to some forms of the more current "restructured schools", the history of schooling gives many examples of school organisations that may help sustain democratic pedagogy. The difficulty for these reforms has not been in producing alternative pedagogies, but in sustaining them.

If there is but one reason to applaud the current wave of educational restructuring, it is that within the broad current agenda of school restructuring (a highly contradictory and internally varied movement in itself) there are many attempts around the globe to find ways of making democratic school reforms stick, to find ways of embedding democratic learning within our largely bureaucratic school systems. In Australia, the most obvious national examples of such reforms can be found within the work of the National Schools Network, where many schools have attempted to reorganise teaching and learning to increase students' self-guided participation in their own learning (and teachers' participation in organising their work). In the United States, similar examples can be found among the schools in the Coalition of Essential Schools, where there is a very similar commitment to restructure schools on the basis of what teachers know to be good, democratic pedagogy. More specific Australian examples can be found among the current moves to reorganise middle schooling by building curricula based on students' own collective interests and stated goals.

Perhaps one of the most important things to note about such restructuring efforts is that research has already been able to demonstrate that such schooling not only improves learning outcomes, but does so much more equitably than any traditional schooling ever has. That is, in a series of national studies of restructuring schools in the United States, the former Center on Organization and Restructuring of Schools at the University of Wisconsin-Madison has shown that schools which have a strong focus on learning that emphasises (a) students constructing their own knowledge, through (b) disciplined inquiry and substantive conversation, where what the students learn has (c) value beyond the school, all students learn more and learn more equitably than in both "less authentic" restructuring schools and traditionally organised schools (Newmann and Wehlage 1995). It is probably very important to note that these democratic restructuring schools are a *very* small minority in the United States. For democratically minded teachers, it is also important to note that these schools were able to generate such learning more easily with a strong, professional, collaborative community of teachers.

Obviously such research may not readily translate into the Australian context. (There are many systemic differences between the United States and Australia when it comes to school systems and teachers' work.) However, combined with the strong tradition of democratic curriculum and teaching in Australia, it is safe to say that democratic Australian educators have a fair idea of where to begin the attempt to build more democratic school systems.[4]

In a general sense then, democratic educators have begun to construct the knowledge needed to make current institutions work differently. Simply put, however, for many of these necessary proposals, we simply do not know how to do it systemically over long periods of time, for all students. Consequently, the need to continue the fundamental struggle for finding ways to embed democratic education into our daily school lives remains.

While many of these issues are, for educators, technical questions of how to organise and run schools, other less technical questions also need to be addressed. After all, many, many issues of education and schooling are not settled by technical knowledge. Much of education remains an all-out, pure political battle. Let us be clear and forthright here. If Australia is to develop democratic forms of schooling, some very difficult ideo-logical and political battles will need to be fought. For the remainder of this discussion we would like to address some of the outstanding debates that will need to be addressed in the politics of schooling, in the political understandings of public institutions more generally, and in the overall development of an Australian democratic public will.

Lessons from the politics of schooling

> What the best and wisest parent wants for his [sic] own child, that must the community want for all its children. Any other ideal is narrow and unlovely; acted upon, it destroys our democracy. (Dewey 1968: 3)

Democratic struggles in schooling have long held various notions of equity as a standard or ideal against which educational politics could be assessed. We accept this position whole-heartedly and unashamedly. If Australia could hold but one educational achievement up to international scrutiny, we believe it can and should be the degree to which educational equity has been accepted and defended as a common educational good in Australia.

The language of equity, however, can be very slippery; and there are signs that Australian educators have succumbed to some of the same

---

4   Specific examples of schooling practices which have been shown to produce more democratic outcomes are reported, for instance, in Apple and Beane (1996), Darling-Hammond (1996), and Newmann and Associates (1996).

misguided notions of equity that can be found in other parts of the world – most notably the United States. Here we would simply point out the need to guard against distortions of equity and social justice within the politics of education. For example, it is common in the public debates of the United States to find people saying educational equity means nothing more than allowing individual students to "reach their full individual" potential. This is a very beguiling and highly misleading idea, for it replaces the democratic appeal to a public, common will with an individualistic ethic that is ultimately, by definition, selfish.

For example, at the risk of alienating many parents, to argue that "gifted and talented" programs are responsive to students who have been "disadvantaged" in schools, on the grounds that an equitable school should cater for all students to their individual "potential", is to argue for more resources for students who are, by and large, already doing quite well in school. There may be many reasons to argue for such programs, and how they work does, in fact, vary tremendously from place to place (making such broad generalisations as the one we just advanced risky). For us, however, to argue in support of such programs on the grounds of "equity" is both misleading and dishonest (not to mention empirically unsound: to our knowledge, available evidence does not consistently support the idea that such programs help anyone any more than democratic forms of schools). It is not the responsibility of any democratic collective to guarantee the fulfilment of individual potential, nor should eliminating barriers to individual advancement be misconstrued to mean providing resources for advancement into positions of unequally high power.

In the overall politics of schooling, such political moves are to us clearly part of a larger politics of resentment. Other examples of the politics of resentment are all too common. Where advocates of boys' education point to the resource base given to the advancement of girls' and women's education, and argue that a "fair share" is due to "the boys", clearly a sense of public hostility and selective interest is raised. There are many good reasons to worry about boys' education and masculinity; but to do so by suggesting that what we have been able to achieve for girls and women is somehow "unfair" is to denigrate one of the few educational policy successes of the 20th century.

Similar lessons have been learned from studies of race, ethnicity and multiculturalism. It is quite clear that educating for tolerance, and specialised programs designed only for the "targeted minority", often fail to address broader issues of racism for the entire population. The current public backlash against Australia's indigenous peoples demonstrates the need for a broad-band anti-racist education that might mitigate misplaced public resentment. Simply put, a public education program on the nature of educational equity also needs to remain on the political agenda.

The politics of public institutions and a common will

Obviously this image of schooling is radical compared to the schools that currently exist in Australia today; but this image poses radical reform of other public institutions well beyond schooling. The guiding principles of social justice that underpin education also apply to other public institutions. If we work from the now classical framework of justice posed by the liberal philosopher John Rawls (1971), for example, we can note that public institutions (including the legal bases of economics, as well as other more visible public provisions) can be assessed with two simple principles:

1. that "each person is to have an equal right to the most extensive basic liberty compatible with a similar liberty for others", and
2. that "social and economic inequalities are to be arranged so that they are both a) reasonably expected to be to everyone's advantage, and b) attached to positions and offices open to all" (p 60).

In understanding public institutions, this second principle translates into the now famous notion that whatever inequalities are accepted need to "most advantage the least advantaged". A minimal essential education (along with other basic provisions such as health and welfare), in this formulation, would mostly be defended by reference to the first principle of maximising and protecting "basic liberties", since such an education would be necessary to exercise liberties. Other public institutions would face the second criterion more often. Here we have to begin asking some tough questions, such as: What good would a minimal essential education for democracy do if there were to be only private economic control over the media (and hence only distorted information widely available)? or How could everyone seriously participate in a democracy predicated on a minimal essential education, if access to professions were to be affordable only to those able to pay outright for professional higher education? or What good does critical literacy do if you can't get a job?

Clearly here we are attempting to raise some very important issues which need current, public, intelligent debate. While governments throughout the world rapidly attempt to maximise their nations' economic income, we have to ask at what cost will that maximisation come? and Who will ultimately benefit from any increased economic productivity? If maximising economic output means guaranteeing a large pool of unemployed people will continue to be out of work, is that just? If making labour more productive means inter-professional competition for whatever salary increase might be won, will that most benefit the least advantaged? And if the current focus on economic gains is played out by basically trading away basic health, education, and welfare provisions, who stands to gain? Simply put, if democratic educators are to reorganise their schools and encourage students to openly question their own learning, we can be sure these students will begin to ask what justice they are to face when they walk out the school door. Without even considering issues of hypocrisy, the likely rude fact remains that democratic educators will only be able to instil democratic virtues in students to the degree that a thriving, just democracy exists in the wider society, in the world.

Education and wider social policies are often difficult to explain in public. In Australia, however, there are public precedents for the foundation of a just social democracy. Key elements of current social policy in Australia seem worth protecting. Rather than being satisfied with the more American preoccupation with making everything equal for individuals at "the start" of public life (that is, when children are only five years old), Australia has a tradition of developing policies based on a commitment to equality of outcomes. In our current, rapidly advancing, technological Australia, this seems only wise. If Australia drops its vigilant watch on the outcomes of our public institutional systems, the stark inequalities of the United States might well migrate across the Pacific, south. Although cliche to many ears, Australia's sense of a "fair go" may well be at risk in the current educational climate, and a democratic education for all may well be a significant linchpin in any public demand for maintaining that uniquely Australian, socially just "fair go".

References

Apple, M.W. and J.A. Beane (eds) (1996) *Democratic Schools*. Alexandria, Virginia: Association for Supervision and Curriculum Development.

Bernstein, B. (1990) *The Structuring of Pedagogic Discourse: Volume 4: Class, Codes and Control*. London: Routledge.

Darling-Hammond, L. (1996) "The Right to Learn and the Advancement of Teaching: Research, Policy, and Practice for Democratic Education". *Educational Researcher*, 25 (6), 5-17.

Dewey, J. (1916) *Democracy and Education*. New York: Free Press.

Dewey, J. (1968) *The School and Society*. Chicago: University of Chicago Press.

Gore, J.M. (1995) "On the Continuity of Power Relations in Pedagogy". *International Studies in Sociology of Education*, 5(2), 165-188.

Gutman, A. (1987) *Democratic Education*. Princeton, New Jersey: Princeton University Press.

Johnston, S. (1990) *Retention Rates: More than Just Counting Heads*. Queensland: Department of Education.

Newmann, F. and Associates (1996) *Authentic Achievement: Restructuring Schools for Intellectual Achievement*. San Francisco: Jossey Bass Publishers.

Newmann, F. and G. Wehlage (1995) *Successful School Restructuring*. Madison, Wisconsin: Center on Organization and Restructuring of Schools.

Rawls, J. (1971) *A Theory of Justice*. Cambridge, Massachusetts: Harvard University Press.

Teese, R. et al (1995) *Who Wins at School? Boys and Girls in Australian Secondary Education*. Canberra: AGPS.

Young, I.M. (1990) *Justice and the Politics of Difference*. Princeton: Princeton University Press.

3

What qualities of citizenship should Australian schools emphasise?

Lucas Walsh and Mike Salvaris

Linking citizenship to schooling

The definition and experience of Australian citizenship has gained greater significance in recent years as Australia approaches the centenary of its federation amidst national and global transformation. Nationally, the pace of debate about our future constitutional structure is quickening as the likelihood of an Australian republic increases. Across the world we see the playing out of the dangerous ideological tension between citizenship as stolid, municipal and dutiful on the one hand; and citizenship as a critical, democratic, equalising, and potentially revolutionary aspect of culture on the other. Against this backdrop it is challenging to consider possible directions for citizenship in Australia.

In this chapter we will discuss some of the ways in which education is able to define Australian culture. In particular, we wish to highlight the linkages between schooling and the quality of democratic society through the learning and teaching of citizenship. We will explore and diagnose the present and past developments of citizenship education in schools and analyse new directions in citizenship education for the future.

Our conception of citizenship is based upon an ideal or desirable type. This ideal type of democratic citizenship includes the education of active, critical, and politically literate citizens. The active, democratic citizen ought to have a well developed sense of civic ethic or duty within a concept of citizenship that emphasises community/social solidarity in a broader framework of good international citizenship practices. Crucial to the concrete definition of desirable citizenship for Australian practice is the implementation of standards, benchmarks and indicators.

Given their current organisation, schools are imperfect models for democracy and citizenship. Furthermore, the state's approach to citizenship education in schools is one of ambivalence between rhetorical and actual commitment to ideas like democracy and citizenship. We argue that only weak models of citizenship will be transmitted in schools while this ambivalence dominates the state's commitment to ideas like democracy and citizenship. With these limitations in mind, we attempt to locate the possible links between schooling and citizenship through the identification of potential or theoretical approaches and resources that schools have to teach democratic citizenship. These approaches include the teaching of citizenship as history, as a set of political institutions and as a vocation, and the development of the school as a model/example of a democratic civic community.

We also explore new directions and possibilities for schooling for active democratic citizenship. Our contention is that if we are to be fully committed to teaching this model of citizenship, new approaches to citizenship education will need to be developed. Our approach emphasises the use of practical models within the school and local community to engage democratic processes including pedagogical and institutional strategies aimed at areas such as curriculum, teaching method and the conception of the school as a democratic civic community.

What is a desirable form of citizenship?

The ancient Greeks believed that man (sic) is by nature a political animal, and it was in Athens that democracy was conceived. Democracy in Ancient Greece was anchored in the Greek concept of the "citizen". But citizenship meant that only men of strict Athenian or Spartan background could participate in public affairs: have an active role in public meetings, vote, give judgement or hold office (Held 1987: 1-3). Slaves and women did not have a say in government.

Eclipsed by Christianity, democracy re-emerged in the English language in the 16th century. Classical liberal thinkers of the day advocated a limited notion of citizenship because they were wary of what they saw as the potential for mass participation to develop into "mob rule". Held (1987: 3) notes how classical liberal thinkers attempted to "restrict the meaning of 'the people' to certain groups: among others, owners of property, white men, educated men, men, those with particular skills ..." The principles of classical liberalism implied that certain citizens enjoy political equality in order that they be free to rule and be ruled in turn. This doctrine of citizenship was based on the assumption that human beings are essentially self-interested. Therefore, freedom meant the securing of the privacy of individuals to pursue their chosen interests (Held 1987: 34).

Oldfield (1990: 177-87) contrasts liberal individualism, in which citizenship is conceived in terms of legal *status*, to the emphasis of civic republicanism on the *practice* of citizenship for the common good. Within the republican conception of citizenship, active citizenship in political life is the highest form of active life because the public good surpasses the good of any particular individual (Williams 1995: 135). Today, liberals are still divided on whether a viable community can be maintained in the long run if individuals are to be viewed as simply self-interested (Emy and Hughes 1988: 188-89).

According to Giddens, citizenship took its most important form in the bourgeoisie's class struggle to escape feudal domination. The development of modern citizenship is linked to the expansion of state sovereignty and the build-up of administrative power from the late 16th century, which included an increased ability of the state to survey its subjects and to rely on cooperative forms of social relations. Nationalism was also a critical force in the development of democratic citizenship, or what Giddens calls the "cultural sensibility of sovereignty" (Giddens in Held 1989: 196-197).

In this century, citizenship has come to mean full membership of a distinct political community. Marshall (1950) defined this membership in terms of the participation by individuals in the determination of the conditions of their own association. Citizenship is a status bestowing upon individuals equal rights and duties, liberties and constraints, powers and responsibilities. According to the Senate Legal and Constitutional References Committee (SLCRC):

> What are conventionally described as political, civil and social rights all denote broadly distinct categories of entitlements that can be attached to citizenship. (SLCRC 1995: 11)

Marshall contended that while there is no universal principle that determines what exactly the citizen's rights and duties shall be, societies create an image of an "ideal citizenship" and, thereby, "a goal towards which aspirations can be directed" (Held 1989: 190).

Contemporary theorists of citizenship are tending to move away from a view of citizenship as a nationalistic concept and are moving towards a view of citizenship based on ideas like human rights. For example,

Habermas observes that the republican conception of citizenship "completely parts company with the idea of belonging to a pre-political community integrated on the basis of descent, a shared tradition and a common language . . ." Within this republican conception, "citizens wish to organise their peaceful coexistence in line with principles which meet with the justified agreement of all because they are in the equal interest of all" (Habermas 1992: 3-5). In the Australian context the development of citizenship is also marked by the playing out of the ideological tension between citizenship as impassive, dutiful membership and citizenship as critical, pro-active and inclusive.

The meanings of Australian citizenship

In Australia, citizenship is generally taken to refer to the status of nationality and the rules and laws which govern that status, like the right to passports and the right to vote. Barrett (1995) observes that the Australian notion of citizenship is primarily a legal one, in which the citizen has various rights and duties in respect to political participation, such as voting, land ownership and travel outside of national boundaries. While the formal and legal status of citizenship is defined in the *Australian Citizenship Act* 1948, James (1994) concludes that much of the formal notion of citizenship in Australia hasn't developed much since the 19th century.

Beneath the formal definition of citizenship is a much broader and more social notion that takes citizenship to mean the quality of full membership and active participation in a just, democratic and mutually supportive political community. Rights and duties must have community support reflecting the context and actual experience of citizenship – "rights have as a corollary duties to respect the enjoyment of rights by others" (SLCRC 1995: 14). According to Kymlicka and Norman (1994):

> Citizenship is not just a certain status, defined by a set of rights and responsibilities. It is also an identity, an expression of one's membership in a political community. (p 352)

Here is a broader notion of the democratic citizen who participates in government to guarantee liberty through the cultivation of civic virtues and devotion to the common good (Mouffe 1992; Leca 1992). Here also we see the ongoing tension between the idea of citizenship as a narrowly prescribed legal status defining relations between individual and state, and citizenship as a broader process of social and civic participation.

Citizens have to believe that they have an active involvement in political decision-making processes (Emy and Hughes in Hague et al 1993). Yet, according to Mackay (1993), Australians:

> have been plunged into a period of unprecedented social, cultural, political, economic and technological change, in which the Australian way of life is being radically redefined.

In contemporary Australia, there is little doubt that there has been a movement of power towards the Federal government and away from most citizens, due, in part, to the insulation of expert policy-making and law-making from popular pressure (Walker 1993; Evans in Walker et al 1993).

Democratic standards of freedom are increasingly determined within the narrow discourse of economic rationalism. The relationship of the citizen to the state has been recast in terms of a "user-pays" mentality which aggrandises the state as a service provider, and a "clientelisation" of the citizen (Turner in SLCRC 1995; see also Habermas 1992). The intense pressures of competitive individualism and consumerism, utilitarianise social values to the point where they produce pathological side effects in social relations, such as gross class inequality (Pusey 1987). According to Castles (1985), citizenship has evolved as a function of the "wage-earners' welfare state" in which the full benefits and status of citizenship are only available to male (mostly white) wage-earners. He argues that this narrow conception excludes or marginalises other citizens with legitimate interests and civic claims in their own right, such as women and the unemployed, as well as helping to sustain racist and exclusionary policies. Under this confined economic liberal view of citizenship, the average citizen is treated more as a client of the state rather than as an active, participating member in the democratic life of the nation.

Historically, Australians have thought of themselves as strongly egalitarian, which can be seen every day in "mateship" and the belief in giving every one a "fair go". These are important components of citizenship. But there has been a decline in some practical indicators of social equity, sharper differences in income and wealth, and growing levels of poverty (especially among women). A senate committee reported that there has been a "decline in civic values as evidenced by marked increases in the sense of personal alienation, powerlessness and a diminished sense of community" (SLCRC 1995: 6). Australians have come to increasingly rely on economic indicators to measure social wellbeing: "Older images [of national identity] have been replaced by the more abstract idea of 'the economy' " (Horne in SLCRC 1995: 26). There is evidence to suggest that many Australian citizens, especially young people, are experiencing a loss of direction and a growing feeling of isolation (Mackay 1993). Consequently, "these circumstances suggest the need for some reappraisal of citizenship, national identity and community goals" (SLCRC 1995: 6).

The current state of Australian citizenship is, therefore, problematic. For citizenship to be meaningful in a democracy, the citizen must be active, critical and politically literate, possessing a well developed civic ethic or sense of civic duty. Teaching civics and citizenship in schools requires a clear and popularly recognised sense of what legitimate and effective democratic citizenship means at a practical level.

Standards, indicators, audits and benchmarks

In 1995, the SLCRC concluded that any rational approach to citizenship reform may need to focus on establishing a clear definition of the basic rights and duties of individual citizens and standards in at least those policy areas that are necessary to sustain social participation and social wellbeing. It was suggested that standards of effective citizenship need to be developed to provide a unifying theme based on widely accepted values and symbols "such as democracy, fairness, tolerance, participation and social solidarity" which "may be the key to keeping a diverse and multicultural society together" (SLCRC 1995: 10). The committee argued that a careful consideration of the most effective ways to implement these rights, duties and policy standards in government and community could be achieved through legislation, charters, rights and national policy standards (SLCRC 1995: 15).

Both Deakin University and the Centre for Urban and Social Research at Swinburne University are currently developing separate audits of Australian democracy. Typically, audits attempt to provide a framework for evaluating the quality and effectiveness of democratic values, institutions and citizenship in Australia. In 1995, Glen Withers, the director of the Federal Government's Economic Planning Advisory Commission, advocated a democratic audit to establish the basis for the expansion of direct participation, which, through mass education and advanced information technology, could ensure more just economic outcomes (Withers in Fagan 1995: 6).

Because social benchmarks and indicators of citizenship are not well developed, Australians have come to depend on economic indicators as poor surrogates. A citizenship charter, which could be implemented instead of a United States-style bill of rights, would outline Australia's national goals and values, acting as a guide to general policy (SLCRC 1995). A charter may include national social benchmarks and policy standards in key areas of public policy, monitored by a set of national indicators.

Hattam (1995) argues that benchmarking democratic practice as well as economic wellbeing is necessary to curb the erosion of social services, such as public education, currently taking place across Australia. Specifically, an audit of democratic practice would:

1. benchmark social indicators in areas such as education,
2. actively seek participation from the most silenced and oppressed groups in society in the auditing process, and
3. use the process to enliven debates about Australia's democratic future.

Hattam proposes some possible benchmarks in the arena of teachers' work as a manageable way of beginning a broader audit of democracy.

Rights and civic duties

At the most basic level, there must be a formal representation of citizenship embodied in law and policy to provide a democratic frame of reference by which possibly negative encroachments may be identified and evaluated (Salvaris 1996). Rights are one of the key ways in which citizenship may be defined because they form and shape the nature of membership of a political community. Held (1989) defines rights as:

> legitimate spheres of independent action (or inaction) . . . The autonomy of the citizen can be represented by that bundle of rights which individuals can enjoy as a result of their status as "free and equal" members of society (pp 200-201).

Held also outlines four spheres of rights – civil, political, economic and social rights – which would provide the basic ground rules that make democracy possible. But again, there are tensions in the ways in which different ideological groups see how political rights should be expressed. For example, liberal democrats want rights to express individual freedom more fully, while social democrats believe in constraining some individual freedom in the interest of the collective good.

Rights are of little use if they are not actively enjoyed (Pateman 1970). Participatory theory advocates a model of democratic citizenship in which there is a high degree of ongoing citizen involvement with social justice issues and in various organisations. Participatory theorists:

> argue for democratisation and politicization of small scale associations in which individuals could play a significant role [placing] emphasis on institutions other than those of the central government (Lively 1990: 140-141).

This points to the need for a wide degree of democratic participation in many spheres of life, from the classroom to the workplace, to encourage:

> the belief that one can be self-governing, and [have] confidence in one's ability to participate responsibly and effectively, and to control one's life and environment . . . (Pateman 1970: 46)

Recent reports of government agencies and movements for democratic change agree that reforms to citizenship need to focus on the ethical content of citizenship – especially the idea of civic duty. Civic duty means that individuals and groups must be able to actively and knowledgeably participate in the governance of the political community in which they are members. Essential to civic duty is that all citizens take responsibility in the public interest. This in turn requires a sense of solidarity and belonging. A key assumption is that people have the desire or will to become involved in the political life of the nation. Oldfield (1990) appropriately points out that a belief in the capacity of humanity to participate in democratic life is a vital component of political life in a democracy. Without this core belief, any theory which claims to be arguing for democracy is emptied of its validity.

Education makes citizens

The French historian and politician Alexis de Tocqueville observed in the early 19th century that schools were an important democratic institution in which men (sic) had the opportunity to rise above narrow, self-interested world views to pursue activities in the public good (Lively 1990). While still seen as a means of expanding the possibilities for social mobility, modern western public schooling since the late 1960s has attracted widespread criticism, ranging from Illich's (1976a) claim that "[i]n the shadow of each national school-pyramid, an international caste system is wedded to an international class structure" (p 154), to Harraway's (1991) conclusion that education since the 1980s has perpetuated "mass ignorance and repression in technocratic and militarised culture" (p 171).

The intimate link between the quality of mass education and the quality of democracy places the school in a crucial and oftentimes precarious position in shaping the democratic wellbeing of society. The bearing of public education on political, social and economic wellbeing is significant because of the popular recognition of the school as a key site for the development of social cohesion and identity among Australians as students, teachers, workers, entrepreneurs and democratic citizens. A pivotal connection between the school, citizenship and democracy is citizenship education.

The meanings of civics and citizenship education

Civics education concerns the instruction, study and learning of citizenship and the rights and duties of each citizen within a democratic polity. Traditionally, civics education has two overlapping functions:

1. to provide information to citizens about national identity and its historical development, and
2. to provide information about civic life, politics and government.

According to the Civics Expert Group (CEG), civics *education* "should address the needs of school students and others in the community" (CEG 1994: 1). The goal of civics education identified by the group "was to ensure that Australians can participate fully in civic decision-making processes" as part of formal education in schools and the promotion of citizenship for the broader community (CEG 1994: 5-7). Given that schooling occurs predominantly within state-controlled or regulated institutions, there are several limitations to teaching democratic citizenship as part of formal schooling.

One of the policies of the former Keating Government was to increase citizenship education in schools, among migrants and in the general community:

> This, in turn [it was argued] will lead to knowledgeable citizens who are equipped to participate in the exercise of the rights and responsibilities which they, as Australian citizens, share. (Department of Immigration and Ethnic Affairs 1995: 3)

The objective of these reforms was to increase the involvement or inclusion of citizens from a variety of different backgrounds into the broader society. Yet, at the time of writing, little progress has been made in the development of citizenship education in Australia.

Civics education in Australian schools has been surpassed by the ideology of vocationalism that has predominated in educational policy making since the Dawkins era of the 1980s. This orientation of public education towards purely economic imperatives is linked to clientelisation of citizenship. The economic rationalisation of formal public education reached a new plateau in 1988, when the Federal Government announced a new education policy emphasising the role of schools in restructuring the national economy and the need to prepare students for a more highly skilled, adaptive and productive workforce. The Dawkins era lead to vast reforms, tailoring education to the economic interests of the nation. The Mayer, Finn and Carmichael reports explored ways in which the education system might be changed to equip students with vocational skills directly relevant to employers.

Benchmarking civics education

In the United States, standards for civics education have been outlined in the National Standards for Civics (McREL 1995 and 1996). The Mid-continent Regional Educational Laboratory (McREL) drew upon these standards in their attempt to provide a comprehensive set of benchmarks for civic and citizenship education (McREL 1995). These included *National Standards for Civics and Government* (1994) from the Centre for Civic Education, *Civitas: A Framework for Civic Education* (Quigly and Bahmmeller 1991), and a series of civics units authored by Law in a Free Society (McREL 1995). In these documents, essential ideas in civics are grouped within over 70 content standards. Each content standard has associated with it a set of key concepts that students should know in order to meet the standard. This approach "seeks to provide content knowledge that is either declarative, procedural, or contextual" and specific resources for teachers and curriculum developers. Emphasising the understanding by all citizens of ideas about civic life, politics and government, these civics standards include the learning of:

- the essential characteristics of limited and unlimited governments,
- the sources, purposes, and functions of law, and the importance of the rule of law for the protection of individual rights and the common good,
- the concept of a constitution, the various purposes that constitutions serve, and the conditions that contribute to the establishment and maintenance of constitutional government,
- the major characteristics of systems of shared powers and of parliamentary systems,

- the role of diversity in American life and the importance of shared values, political beliefs, and civic beliefs in an increasingly diverse American society,
- the meaning of citizenship in the United States, and the requirements for citizenship and naturalisation,
- issues regarding personal, political, and economic rights,
- how certain character traits enhance citizens' ability to fulfil personal and civic responsibilities, and
- how participation in civic and political life can help citizens attain individual and public goals (McREL 1996).

Within these standards, McREL divides United States education into four tiers of schooling. At level one, civics education in the primary sector aims to educate students to develop an awareness of authority, for example, by illustrating situations in which individuals are acting on their own (eg, two friends decide to do something) and situations in which individuals' actions are directed by others (eg, parents tell their children to do something). McREL argues that students should be able to differentiate the use of power with legitimate authority (eg, a teacher tells a group of students to do something) from use of power without authority (eg, an older, larger student tells a group of younger students to do something) and the problems that might result from lack of effective authority (eg, inability to settle disputes or accomplish necessary tasks).

At the upper elementary level, civics education encourages an awareness of various people and groups who make, apply, and enforce rules and laws for others (eg, adult family members, teachers, city councils, national governments) and who manage disputes about rules and laws (eg, courts). The student is expected to know the difference between power (eg, the capacity to control something or someone) and authority (eg, power that people have the right to use because of custom, law, or the consent of the governed), as well as the ways in which authority is used (eg, parents have authority to direct and control their children, governors of states have the authority to carry out and enforce laws) and ways in which power can be used without authority. The student is also expected to have a firm grasp of the basic purposes of government (eg, to protect the rights of individuals, to promote the common good).

At level three (middle school / junior high school) civics education aims to enable the student to distinguish between private life and civic life and how politics enables people with differing ideas to reach binding agreements (eg, presenting information and evidence, stating arguments, negotiating, compromising, voting). The student is expected to learn about institutions that have the authority to direct or control the behaviour of members of a society (eg, a school board, State legislature, courts,). At the high school level, civics education is expected to show how politics enables a group of people with varying opinions and/or interests to reach collective decisions, influence decisions, and accomplish goals that they could not reach as individuals (eg, managing the distribution of resources, allocating benefits and burdens, managing conflicts) (McREL 1996).

These descriptions of standards identify a possible content for civics education. We must now consider how likely it is that the schools and students can engage effectively with this content.

The limitations of formal education

Illich argues that obligatory schooling encourages a false ideology that perpetuates class stratification because of the market value attached to formal qualifications. Illich is critical of the view that school systems provide the means to self-empowerment because the means to public education have become ends in themselves. The development of the education system has become synonymous with education itself, rather than being understood as an institutional arrangement that produces education: "The goals of development are always and everywhere stated in terms of consumer value packages ... and therefore always and everywhere imply more privileges for a few" (Illich 1976a: 147-148). The economic rationalisation of the school induces a user-pays mentality which clientalises the student in the same way as the economic rationalisation of citizenship illustrated above.

In Illich's view, schooling encourages the domestication of citizens through the "slotting" of students into assessment categories and dated didactic teaching strategies" (Illich 1976a). Despite recent government initiatives to stimulate active participation through civics and citizenship education, "the reality of classroom life in Australian schools is that traditional, didactic teaching strategies predominate" (Print 1996). The teaching of values like tolerance, multiculturalism and equality are somewhat hollow in the authoritarian structures that predominate in most modes of learning in public schools. Willis writes that the whole structure of the classroom speaks of hierarchies of oppression. In his seminal study English schools, Willis sums up the influence of the structure of the classroom in this way:

In a simple physical sense school students, and their possible views of the pedagogic situation, are subordinated by the constricted and inferior space they occupy. Sitting in tight ranked desks in front of the larger teacher's desk; deprived of private space themselves . . . all of these things help to determine a certain orientation to the physical environment and behind that a certain kind of social organisation. They speak of the whole position of the student. (Willis 1978: 67-68)

Willis argues that this social organisation of the school reinforces patterns of social domination through "visible staff hierarchies" that monopolise knowledge.

Pedagogical limitations

The form of civics education is as important as its content in the learning of democratic citizenship. By form, we refer to civics pedagogy. Pedagogy is appropriately understood as "the way that subject-matter is selected, organised and presented to learners in an educational context so that teachers can accomplish their educational intentions" (Print 1996).

Traditionally, civics and citizenship education is characterised by class-based, school-based, teacher-centred methods which rely on passive-learning on the part of students. Illich (1976a) argues that the popular belief that most learning is a result of teaching is an illusion. He writes:

Teaching may contribute to certain kinds of learning under certain circumstances. The strongly motivated student faced with the task of learning a new code may benefit greatly from the discipline we now associate mostly with the old-fashioned schoolmaster. But most people acquire most of their insight, knowledge, and skill outside of school . . . (p 154-155)

While citizenship education needs to be oriented towards more student-centred strategies and based on positive views of student learning through participation, teacher-centred strategies are not without some value. There has been a broad body of research since the 1980s indicating the effectiveness of teacher-centred strategies. Teachers *can* provide valuable foundation knowledge and appropriate teaching resources, without which student-centred strategies of civics and citizenship education "can easily become a pool of directionless, ineffective attempts at learning" (Print 1996).

Standards and benchmarks of effective citizenship education may also provide direction to the development of citizenship education. Alongside the necessity for a clearer definition of the values, rights and duties of democracy, citizenship education requires a greater emphasis on participation by student/citizens, both, in and out of school.

New directions – schooling for active democratic citizenship

Civics education of the participatory kind advocated by the Civics Expert Group will not necessarily foster active citizens in tomorrow's democracy. By appealing to historical and culturally-biased conceptions of democratic citizenship, current approaches to civics and citizenship education fail to engage the dynamic relationship of citizens, states, groups and institutions which is constantly reconstituting the political cultures, values and patterns of equality and domination among citizens and their representatives.

Many proposals for civics reform, such as the Civics Expert Group's (1994) report *Whereas the People*, fail to account for changing political cultures and institutions intrinsic to the development of citizenship by appealing to historical values and institutions of democratic politics. Neo-liberal conceptions of citizenship have become widely integrated into everyday political life because they appeal to the philosophical tradition of utilitarianism as a basis for qualifying what they claim to be "true" democratic principles and institutional arrangements. Conservative republican approaches to citizenship education like that of the Civics Experts Group (1994) inappropriately return to traditional democratic values in the face of social change. The Macintyre Report makes these kinds of appeals to respect the historical development of democracy: the discourse of citizenship education becomes limited to certain values which are either outdated or have the potential to restrict the exploration of new and innovative democratic improvements that are applicable to changing political, economic and social contexts. These appeals may unintentionally legitimate the antiquated and culturally defined values and institutions emanating from the republican tradition, fostering the ideological justification of patterns of social, political and economic inequality. What was once understood as the "open republic" in these historical terms is better understood as a "cultural republic" or more dangerously, as a kind of religion in its ideological dogma (Davidson 1997). One of the greatest dangers faced by democratic development and its analysis in the late 20th century is that individuals are increasingly being reduced to cultural, statistical or historical generalisations (or to combinations of these).

Participatory pedagogies

Citizenship education must begin early. Role playing using democratic problem-solving can be used to teach students how to define and overcome conflicts and problems democratically. For example, these procedures could use constitutional reform issues as a real-life case study of how citizens should make their own democratic governance (or perhaps, how they don't get to participate in governance). This could include discussion of voting and getting young people to define their idea of human rights and duties in school. Within the classroom, participatory pedagogics could involve group problem-solving exercises during which students work together to identify the issues or resolve the problems. The teacher can guide students through activities requiring active student participation.

Strategies for effective citizenship education require the development of citizenship education pedagogies that foster critical thinking, particularly through group work, simulations, role play, the use of technology and a variety of other cooperative learning strategies involving group problem-solving exercises. Giroux argues for a critical pedagogy enabling students to become more critically aware of:

> the various ways in which representations are constructed as a means of comprehending the past through the present in order to legitimate and secure a particular view of the future. (Giroux 1991: 19)

While Print (1996) refers specifically to computer technologies such as CD Rom, according to Giroux (1996):

> it might be argued that the most important sites of learning today encompass both television and radio airwaves ... the public is increasingly getting educated about politics from sites of learning such as talk radio, that offer a combination of entertainment, ideology, commentary largely ignored by progressives in their analysis of public intellectuals.

Consequently, Giroux argues for a redefinition of what is meant by critical education to include a wider spectrum of sites in the public sphere beyond the traditional sphere of schooling. Giroux asserts that educators;

> need to use the electronic media as a site of learning in which they can combine entertainment with serious commentaries [to] arouse the language and passion of hope through an appeal to the possibilities of what it means to live in a democracy.

There is evidence to suggest that cooperative learning strategies are more effective than the individualistic and competitive models of learning currently predominating throughout Australian schooling (Print 1996). Cooperative learning involves the use of small group engagement in topical discussions, debates and role-playing activities, in which the learning process is shared. Other strategies include the student-run school assembly, the active multicultural day, fieldwork to Parliament House, a meals-on-wheels program within the community, or school council elections. For these activities to be effective, there needs to be a high degree of student involvement which must be seen as relevant to the student's own experiences of political life (Print 1996).

Teachers and citizenship education

For effective citizenship education, Giroux (1996) asserts that the collective knowledge and actions of critical public intellectuals should be pedagogically geared towards educational and political strategies for extending and entrenching the possibilities of democratic public life. It is through a more comprehensive notion of education as a form of cultural production/reproduction that teachers have the potential to utilise knowledge and power to facilitate the enrichment of democracy across diverse sites of learning.

Osborne (1991) identifies nine principles upon which teachers should develop strategies for civics and citizenship education:

1. Teachers have a clearly articulated vision of education.
2. The material being taught is worth knowing and important.
3. Material is organised as a problem or issue to be investigated.
4. Careful, deliberate attention is given to the teaching of thinking within the context of valuable knowledge.
5. Teachers are able to connect the material with student knowledge and experience.
6. Students are required to be active in their own learning.
7. Students are encouraged to share, to build on each other's ideas.
8. Connections are established between the classroom and the outside world.
9. Classrooms are characterised by trust and openness so that students find it easy to participate.

Restructuring the school?

Although clear standards and pedagogical strategies of civics education are crucial to the education of democratic citizenship, a more extensive reform of civics and citizenship education may include the restructuring of schools themselves as key democratic institutions. Public schooling should provide a frame of reference for political participation, the cultivation of civic virtue, and democratic citizenship. The experience of active participation is a valuable form of political education, which has the potential to empower citizens and groups with a greater critical awareness of their own rights and responsibilities as well as .those of others. Research suggests that if there is active participation in a democratic school climate where principles of democracy are operationalised in school decision-making processes, students are more likely to acquire the values and skills of democratic citizenship (Print 1996). Pateman (1970) writes that:

> for maximum participation by all the people, democracy must take place at other spheres in order that the necessary individual attitudes and psychological qualities can be developed. (p 42)

She argues for an extension of participation into the schools and universities themselves as valuable contexts of "social training". Increased awareness of citizenship through civics education and participation in school decision-making processes are ways of learning a variety of qualities of democratic citizenship.

Effective citizenship education needs to emphasise certain civic themes, such as multiculturalism, tolerance, and the celebration of legitimate differences within respect for universal rights and duties. Like Giroux, we advocate a pedagogical project as a means to extend the principles and practices of democracy. These principles include the non-violent pursuit of self-determination, solidarity, economic justice, equity, and racial tolerance which offer the possibility for diverse groups to imagine new forms of community whose educative dimensions impact directly on the renewal of everyday life (Giroux 1996).

Citizenship education for new forms of community

Given the combination of Australia's historical and cultural links with Britain and the United States, and its expanding commercial relationships with Asia, civics education must reflect both local and global community standards of citizenship. The emphasis of early curricula on European history and culture and the simultaneous exclusion of indigenous peoples' history is an example of culturally insensitive procedures that reinforce oppressive hierarchies of exclusion, rather than encouraging inclusive and empowering strategies of citizenship awareness.

Democratic citizenship is legitimate and meaningful when at least the overwhelming majority of citizens derive a sense of political efficacy and self-empowerment from the social arrangements in which political, economic and social equality is actively enjoyed. By "actively enjoyed" we mean that every individual must be prepared, without coercion, to participate in the determination of their personal conditions of existence alongside their fellow citizens. Civics and citizenship education needs to facilitate the learning of cultural literacies of tolerance and mutual understanding to avoid both the dangers of social cleavage and a false generalisation about individuals as a consequence of their perceived economic, historical and/or cultural backgrounds.

Davidson (1997) argues that the essence of democracy is to reject history, because history has the potential to generate mythologies that generate unfair impressions of certain citizens in the present (eg, unfair in that they create the cultural bases of racism, sexism and other prejudicial generalisations). While democracy is about protecting the freedoms enjoyed by people in the present, part of that protection includes the cultural values and traditions which may be adopted by citizens and communities, provided the practise of these cultures does not impinge upon the abilities of others to do the same. In a multicultural society like Australia, achieving this balance is one of the main challenges of democratic citizenship as it approaches the centenary of federation. Nevertheless,

> The centenary of federation presents Australia with a unique opportunity to strengthen our democracy and to discuss ourselves in terms of our liberal democratic beliefs and institutions. We have an opportunity to emphasise questions of active citizenship in a lively civil society. (Horne 1994)

Conclusion

Within the classroom, the possibilities for civics and citizenship education are still in abundance. While the roles of the state, teacher, student and pedagogy are in urgent need of re-evaluation, the classroom can be a valuable forum in which the qualities of democratic citizenship can be discussed, appreciated and learned, ranging from the cultivation of a sense of social inclusion and solidarity, and active participation in the local community, to a greater awareness of the rights and duties attached to democratic citizenship. As the Senate Legal and Constitutional References Committee (1995) noted: "These civic qualities are not just innate: they can be learned and improved" (p 15). To paraphrase the words of Illich, the importance of citizenship education risks the future of democracy on the educability of its citizens (Illich 1976a).

References

Aronowitz, S. and H. Giroux (1985) *Education Under Siege: The Conservative, Liberal and Radical Debate Over Schooling.* South Hadley, Massachusetts: Bergin and Garvey Publishers.

Australian Science and Technology Council (1987) *Education and National Needs: Report to the Prime Minister.* Canberra: AGPS.

Barrett, W. (1995) "Citizenship and the Media". *Res Republica*, 4(2), 17-19.

Berkeley, G. (1991) "Teacher Quality: Why All the Fuss?" *Unicorn*, 17(1), 19-23.

Cappo, Fr D. (1993) *Citizenship and Welfare: Beyond the Republican Debate.* Australia: Australian Catholic Social Welfare Commission.

Castles, F. (1985) *The Working Class and Welfare.* Sydney: Allen and Unwin.

Centenary Advisory Committee (1994) *2001: Report from Australia.* Canberra: AGPS.

Center for Civic Education (1994) *National Standards for Civics and Government.* Center for Civic Education, Calabasas California, at http://civnet.org/teaching/national/toc.html.

Civics Education Group, (1994) *Whereas the People: Civics and Citizenship Education.* Canberra: AGPS.

Cole-Adams, K. (1993) "Soft Sell Goes to School". *Time Australia*, 15 November, no 46, pp 52-55.

Collins, C. (1992) "The Finn Review: Where Has it Come From? Where Is it Taking Us?" *Unicorn*, 18(1), 44-48.

Davidson, A. (1993) "Understanding Citizenship in Australia". *Beyond the Headlines Politics: Australia and the World*, June, no 1, PARC.

Davidson, A. (1997) *From Subject to Citizen: Australian Citizenship in the Twentieth Century.* Cambridge, UK: Cambridge University Press.

Department of Immigration and Ethnic Affairs (1995) *The Ties That Bind: Government Response to the Report by the Joint Standing*

Committee on Migration: Australians All – Enhancing Australian Citizenship. Canberra: AGPS.

Economic Planning Advisory Council (EPAC) (1993) *Education and Training in the 90s.* Canberra: AGPS.

Emy, H. and O. Hughes (1988) *Australian Politics: Realities in Conflict.* London: Macmillan.

Evans, H. (1992) "Citizens' Initiative Versus Constitutional Government". *Legislative Studies*, 7(1), 53-56.

Fagan, D. (1995) "Adviser Critical of Social Democracy". *The Weekend Australian*, November 18-19, p 6.

Fletcher, J. and B. Galligan (1993) *The Australian Rights Project.* Canberra: Australian National University.

Fromm, E. (1971) "Introduction" in I. Illich *Celebration of Awareness.* Great Britain: Pelican Books.

Giroux, H. (1989) *Schooling for Democracy: A Critical Pedagogy in the Modern Age.* London: Routledge.

Giroux, H. (1991) "Border Pedagogy and the Politics of Modernism". *Education and Society*, 9(1), 23-38.

Giroux, H. (1993) "Living Dangerously: Identity Politics and the New Cultural Racism: Towards a Critical Pedagogy of Representation". *Cultural Studies*, 1(1), 1-26.

Giroux, H.A. (1996) "Right Wing Pedagogy". *The Cultural Studies Times*, website, http://zelda.thomson.com/routledge/cst/giroux.html.

Habermas, J. (1992) "Citizenship and National Identity: Some Reflections on the Future of Europe". *Praxis International*, 12(1), 1-19.

Haraway, D. (1991) *Simians, Cyborgs and Women: The Reinvention of Nature.* New York: Routledge.

Hattam, R. (1995) "Auditing Democracy in the Arena of Teachers' Work". *Flinders Institute for the Study of Teaching Newsletter*, no 1, pp 1-4.

Hattam R. (ed) (1995) "What are the Most Significant Issues Facing Public Education in the 1990's?". *Flinders Institute for the Study of Teaching Newsletter*, no 2, pp 1-4.

Held, D. (1989) *Political Theory of the Modern State.* Cambridge: Polity Press.

Illich, I.D. (1971) *A Constitution for Cultural Revolution*, at http://www.cogsci.ed.ac.uk/~ira/illich/texts/const_revolution/const_revolution.html (21/1/96).

Illich, I.D. (1976a) *Celebration of Awareness*, Great Britain: Pelican Books.

Illich, I.D. (1976b) *Deschooling Society*. Great Britain: Pelican Books.

James, P. (1994) "Reconstituting the Nation-State: A Postmodern Republic Takes Shape". *Arena*, no 4, 69-89.

Kymlicka, W. and W. Norman (1994) "Return of the Citizen: Survey of Recent Work on Citizenship Theory". *Ethics*, 104(2), 352-381.

Lively, J. (1990) *Democracy*. Oxford: Basil Blackwell.

Mackay, H. (1993) *Reinventing Australia*. Sydney: Angus and Robertson.

Marshall, T.H. (1950) *Citizenship and Social Class and Other Essays*. Cambridge, UK: Cambridge University Press.

The Mid-continent Regional Educational Laboratory (McREL) (1996) *Civics Standards*, McREL Web Page, http://www.mcrel.org/standards-benchmarks/standardslib/civics-1.html (4/1/96).

Mouffe, C. (ed) (1992) *Dimensions of Radical Democracy: Pluralism, Citizenship, Community*. London: Verso Press.

Oldfield, A. (1990) "Citizenship: An Unnatural Practice?" *Political Quarterly*, vol 161, pp 177-187.

Osborne, K. (1991) *Teaching for Democratic Citizenship*. Toronto: Our Schools / Our Selves Education on Foundation

Pateman, C. (1970) *Participation and Democratic Theory*. Cambridge, UK: Cambridge University Press.

Print, M. (1996) *Pedagogical Strategies for Civics and Citizenship Education*, Curriculum Corporation Home Page, Faculty of Education, University of Sydney, http://www.curriculum.edu.au/civprint.html (24 September 1996).

Pusey, M. (1987) *Jurgen Habermas*. England: Ellis Horwood.

Salvaris, M. (1996) "A Just Republic or Just a Republic? Citizenship, Democracy and Constitutional Reform" in R. Davis (ed) *Citizenship in Australia: Democracy, Law and Society*. Victoria, Australia: Constitutional Centenary Foundation, pp 143-170.

Senate Legal and Constitutional References Committee (1995) *Discussion Paper on a System of National Citizenship Indicators*. Canberra: AGPS.

Dawkins, J. (1987) *Skills for Australia and Education and National Needs*. Canberra: AGPS.

Toohey, J. (1993) "Ideas for Australia". *Journalists, Academics and Public Intellectual Life in Australia*. Melbourne: Monash University.

Turner, B. (1993) *Citizenship and Social Theory*. London: Sage.

Walker, G. (1993) *Constitutional Change in the 1990s: Moves for Direct Democracy*. Senate Occasional Lecture Series, 17 March 1993 (transcript).

Walker, G., E. Ratnapala and W. Kasper (1993) *Restoring the True Republic*. Australia: Centre for Independent Studies.

Williams, G. (1995) "A Republican Tradition for Australia?" *Federal Law Review*, 1(23), 133-148.

Willis, P. (1978) *Learning to Labour: How Working Class Kids Get Working Class Jobs*. London: Saxon House.

4

"It's not easy being Australian"

Education in a multicultural and multi-racist society

Michael Garbutcheon Singh

Australia is a multicultural society, encompassing within the breadth of its ethnic diversity historical moves to incorporate indigenous peoples, the highly visible Anglo-Celtic ethnic groups, immigrants from Europe, Australians of Asian background, refugees from world wars and sojourners from many other places on planet Earth. Australia is a multicultural society, with laws, institutions and policies for giving ethnic minorities and national indigenous groups (specifically Aborigines and Torres Strait Islanders) a voice; for supporting the cultural conditions they need to exercise their freedom; and for protecting them from social vulnerability and economic disadvantage. However, Australia is also a multi-racist, sexist and class-based society in which xenophobia jostles with misogyny to win the hearts and minds of people facing the psychological distresses borne of continuing, long-term economic crises. Moreover, some Australian governments at the local, State and Federal levels continue to act in ways which sanction the vilification of indigenous peoples, Australians of Asian background and immigrant ethnic groups generally. Tough economic times have shown just how precarious a foothold democratic virtues have in Australia.

Efforts to develop education in this multicultural and multi-racist society are directly linked to these contradictory tendencies, as well as the need to reinvent the school curriculum for the significantly changed times in which we are living. In part, the struggles to represent a range of disenfranchised or otherwise marginalised groups – their interests, needs and perspectives – in the curriculum, is a response to the revaluing of school knowledge due to dramatic social and economic changes globally. Increasing global interdependence is transforming what counts as valued school knowledge, for instance challenging curriculum representations of Australia as culturally homogeneous and dependent solely on Britain. Although not always fully appreciated it is the broader changes associated with global restructuring which are shaping the debates between advocates of Aboriginal perspectives and anti-racist teaching in the curriculum and defenders of curricular legacies borne of the British empire. To explore these themes further, this chapter examines four key issues: first, some of the main reasons why it is not easy to construct benchmarks for education; second, how an educational perspective on the Australian nation might become more attentive to the politics of ethnic and indigenous differences; third, important social objectives for education in a multicultural and multi-racist society; and finally, practices by which to judge the achievements of school education in meeting these objectives.

It is uncontroversial to say that schools have the following four functions: teaching students the knowledge and skills they need for productive work; ensuring that students develop the norms and values appropriate to performing different kinds of work; developing students' capacities for transmitting, interpreting and developing society's cultural traditions; and forming students' social consciousness. These are not separate processes, but occur simultaneously in the teaching of all key learning areas. The teaching of literacy has never been just a matter of instruction in the "sounding out" of letters, nor has it been just the development of a positive predisposition to the reading of poetry among students. It has inevitably involved students in reproducing, developing and critiquing literary traditions, as well as forming students' under-standing of themselves in relation to the nation and the peoples in their society (Luke 1988: 123-153; Viswanathan 1995: 431-437).

To examine some of the problems confronting a nation seeking to develop a perspective that is attentive to the politics of indigenous and ethnic minority differences it is insightful to consider the issue of national identity.

Constructing educational benchmarks

It is not easy for everyone to be an Australian. In this section six reasons for this difficulty are identified. Against this background we can appreciate why it is difficult to decide upon what will be the important social objectives for education in our multicultural and multi-racist society.

Lack of distinctiveness

First, the customs that make being Australian distinctive are not easy to identify and for this reason the value given to Australianness has been too little. How can Australian students of Anglo-Celtic ethnicity feel a sense of pride in a flag which celebrates the English annexation of Scotland and colonisation of Ireland? What pride can they take in an anthem celebrating an exclusionary, Protestants-only monarchy? Evidence that Australianness has not been highly valued can be found in the failure to encourage British migrants to become Australian citizens. Similar evidence can be seen in the failure to establish what citizenship means for those born in Australia, including the failure to establish what Australianness means for the Aboriginal, Torres Strait and South Sea Islander peoples. Likewise, questions regarding what migrants can expect of their new country by way of rights and what this country can expect from migrants by way of obligations are rarely given explicit answers. Even where answers are given to these questions they are usually anti-democratic due to their insistence on silence, suppression of cultural identity, and pressure to acquiesce to racism. The ease with which hatred can be incited against Australians of Asian or Aboriginal background, for instance, not only indicates the fragile foothold of democratic virtues in this society but is reinforced by the lack of specific details as to the forms of loyalty expected of them, symbolic or otherwise. Ethnic minority and indigenous groups frequently attempt to clarify and make explicit the basis of an inclusive sense of Australianness through their generation of national symbols. They frequently express the need for one key symbol of national loyalty so as to neutralise intolerance and to take the day-to-day pressure off them having to constantly exhibit loyalty through impossible demands for conformity (Modood 1992).

Questionable values

Second, some of those values that have been identified with being Australian do not make it easy for ethnic minorities or indigenous peoples, let alone Anglo-Celtic ethnics, to feel grateful, loyal or proud. The media replay stereotypical images which stigmatise and marginalise certain ethnic minority groups and reproduce sexist images which eroticise ethnic-minority women (Jakubowicz 1994). The uncertainty surrounding whether such values are fully accepted and have widespread consent is cause for concern among all Australians who see their traditional democratic values of power-sharing, freedom and social justice under attack. Efforts to construct Australianness within a narrow and exclusionary framework which values a "White Australia", British descent and imperial loyalty do not provide a basis for generating objectives appropriate to education in a multicultural society (Macintyre, Boston and Pascoe 1994: 14). Similarly, efforts to promote a sense of Australianness in terms of the values, privileges and benefits of the British aristocracy have not been hugely successful among either Anglo-Australians or other ethnic groups or the peoples colonised by the British. However, counter efforts continue to be made to define Australian values in terms of an inclusive and productive relationship between the government and all Australians, including ethnic minorities and indigenous peoples.

Rejection and discrimination

Third, it is not easy for Australians of certain ethnic minority backgrounds to be recognised and accepted as Australians. Over the years different ethnic minorities have been discriminated against, with some, for instance, having their rights to citizenship or to own property being limited; others have had their entry to selected trades and professions restricted, and still others have been denied access to pensions, public housing or senior jobs in government and business. While the consequences of these past forms of rejection and discrimination continue to affect people's present life situation, many members of ethnic minorities still face barriers of systemic discrimination and institutional failure to respond to their needs. However, ethnic minorities and indigenous peoples cannot be treated as inferiors in work, welfare and education, and still be expected to feel as though they belong to this country. For this reason the concept of "racism" is still of central importance to understanding the everyday structuring of people's lives in Australian society (Vasta and Castles 1995). It takes more than "a racist and a bigot" to divide any one nation — such an individual is a sign of the underlying desires and forces at work within society. Should Australia continue to have as its expressed purpose the pursuit of the interests of the dominant ethno-religious groups, this situation will continue to undermine solidarity between all ethnic and indigenous groups. Where intolerance of cultural differences is turned into social injustice by militant anti-Asian, anti-Aboriginal, anti-migrant interests, the demagoguery of Anglo-ethnic fundamentalism will narrow the curriculum by excluding cultural difference, diverse cultural traditions and multiple identities.

Attacks on the advances that have been made

There is a fourth problem which has not made it easy for ethnic minorities and indigenous peoples to be Australians. It has not been easy for them, and their allies among Anglo-Celtic Australians, to establish, protect and further advance public policies, programs and laws which are attentive to and rejoice in cultural differences. There are frequent attacks on the progress that has been made to advance the freedoms of multicultural Australians, or which seek to advance their rights and obligations to participate in public decision-making, or which seek to protect them from all forms of injustice, including, for example, racial vilification. Government cutbacks in public services frequently target ethnic minorities, migrants, refugees and indigenous Australians. How can we feel proud to be Australians when our political leaders seek to discipline us through increasing income inequalities, lack of job security, high unemployment and low levels of positive welfare provisions? Our leaders have done much to teach us to despise democratic governance in preference for a wild and unregulated market. They have sold off public sector enterprises established for the public good, public assets established for the good of the Australian public. In trying to challenge these attacks on the advances made for the public good, it is not compassion that Australians of Asian or indigenous backgrounds want, but policies which take away the need for compassion, a need that has been caused by current commitments to economic irrationalities.

"One nation" and changing global relations

Given current global restructuring we have to acknowledge a fifth problem associated with being an Australian. The autonomy of Australia as a nation-state has always been constrained by its global inter-dependence. The social objectives for education in a multicultural and multi-racist society must therefore be considered in terms of Australia's global embeddedness. Australia was part of a global system founded on English colonial expansionism and pursued its global interests – in politics and economics – through the British empire, assimilating Anglo and immigrant Australians towards an idealised sense of Englishness. From the Second World War onwards Australia became increasingly enmeshed in the super-power struggles and increasingly dependent on the United States – creating a crisis in immigration policy and the development of multicultural settlement programs. With the disintegration of communist states and the end of the Cold War by the close of the 1980s, Australia has been caught up in and contributing to the global restructuring of movements of finance, technology, ideas, images and people. Now the idea of Australia as "one nation" has to be redeveloped in relation to the mutually reinforcing tendencies of making its cultural diversity productive in new international markets and changes in global interdependence. The mission of schools to educate for a multicultural, anti-racist democracy is at risk due to efforts to make international economic competitiveness and the training of workers the exclusive focus of schooling. Increasing global interdependence is giving rise to worldwide concepts and rules governing people's rights and obligations, and ironically many of these are now being formalised and legitimised by international codes and laws governing trade and commerce.

Ethnic diversity, cultural differences and discontinuities in global connectedness continue to be central issues in Australia's sociopolitical life. The economic turmoil, psychological distresses and the feelings of betrayal being experienced by so many Australians – including Anglo-Australians, Asian-Australians and indigenous Australians – have been brought about by the wilful participation of our governments in the global restructuring of transnational capital. Under the slogan of "globalisation" Australian governments have, for the past decade or more, reduced real wages and the buying power of family incomes; unilaterally removed tariff protections; deregulated controls governing investments by transnational corporations; privatised public assets – our common wealth – in preference to a fair tax system, and reduced support to the nation's farming and manufacturing industries. Concerns about the resulting increases in structural unemployment – the dashing of the hopes of young people and their families – have not been used to generate widespread opposition to governments and their irrational economic reductionist policies, nor has it led to resistance to the new technologies which are creating global unemployment (Noble 1995). Instead, the real causes of these disastrous effects have been sidelined, and scapegoats found in Australians with indigenous and Asian backgrounds. The crisis in government economic policy has been conveniently translated into a struggle over white ethnicity which is being mobilised to engender racial hatred and social divisions across the nation. While hardly an appropriate rationale for any one nation, these circumstances have made it increasingly likely that Australian governments will adopt policies that are "backward, intolerant and extremist".

Lack of leadership and vision

The sixth problem concerns Australia's lack of the societal leadership that would enable schools and teachers to move within and between zones of culture difference and to be attentive to indigenous and ethnic differences. For instance, in recent times we have witnessed a failure of responsibility to exercise political and moral leadership in addressing racial vilification. Australia seems to lack the leadership needed to provide the intellectual and moral map that is so necessary for giving students and their teachers insights into the current state of the post-Cold-War world, and what Australia should be or could become under these new and uncertain circumstances. As well there is an absence of leadership to provide a sense of identification where the needs and concerns of all Australians are shared; there is a preference for appeasing the demands of transnational multimedia corporations, overlooking the anger and frustration of white, middle-class Australia, and forgetting the plight of those made redundant or poor by the economic irrationalities of government policies (see West 1993). This lack of leadership means that the only framework Australians have been provided for interpreting the depressing events and crises they face in their day-to-day lives is racist scapegoating. Few political leaders have come forth to speak without appeals to racism, to the ambivalences of fear and desire the Australian people have towards Australia's changing relations with its indigenous peoples and people from Asia. Neither the economic reductionist agenda for privatising public education nor the parochial and chauvinistic view of schooling have provided an adequate narrative for explaining these changes. The managerial preoccupation with economic indicators, and the use of the privatised marketplace to relegate Australians to the position of consumers, are undermining the efforts of schools to nurture and sustain democracy. Governments seem to be refusing to address the root causes of people's suffering – poverty, unemployment – brought by the changing social, economic and cultural conditions to which they have contributed; instead they are allowing Aborigines and Asians to be scapegoats for the circumstances government policies have created. Is there one perspective on nation that is attentive to the politics of ethnic and indigenous differences? It is this issue that is the focus of the next section.

Nation and the politics of difference

Democracy offers one important perspective on what it means for a nation to be attentive to the politics of ethnic and indigenous differences. By and large the claims on this nation by indigenous and ethnic minorities are not about separatism, but are about redefining its practices, relationships and ideas so as to sustain Australia as one nation. For instance, the contributions of indigenous and ethnic minorities to the debates over Australianness, the nation's flags and its other symbols indicate that these Australians do value their cultural membership of this nation, so much so that they want to be officially recognised as being part of it. The need for adherence to the idea of Australia as one nation means that indigenous groups and ethnic minorities should be part of democracy at work. The virtues of democracy can no longer be the exclusive possession of the dominant ethnic group, social class or any other group. Moreover, because of the give-and-take of democracy, the dominant ethnic, class and gender groups should expect and accept change in Australian society as a result of the contribution of ethnic minorities and indigenous peoples. The challenge is for a rethink of curriculum perspectives on these "Other" Australians, and to teach so that ethnic and indigenous diversity is recognised as being at the core of Australianness; this is what makes this society distinctively Australian. Here then the objective of education is to provide a means to incorporate ethnic and indigenous minorities into one nation in which they are seen to belong and feel as though they belong, based on the democratic principles of power-sharing, social justice and freedom (Kymlicka 1995; Norman 1987).

Ensuring a voice for indigenous and ethnic minority groups

Indigenous and ethnic minorities need to see themselves reflected in educational decision-making bodies; at the very least, this may help to reduce their sense of alienation from the education system and place their questions concerning the legitimacy of particular aspects of it on the public agenda (Kymlicka 1995). More importantly, their representation in educational decision-making is not just appropriate for a nation which proclaims itself to the world as being democratic but is consistent with many features of existing practices for ensuring the representation of stakeholders. The representation of indigenous and ethnic minorities in educational decision-making is a continuation of long-established practices of involving "communities of interest" in such work, including parents and citizens, students, professional associations, education employers, teacher unions and universities. Significantly, this commitment to representing these communities of interest in educational decision-making shows the importance of group representation in democratic educational politics – of representing constituencies based on shared interests rather than geography.

The representation of indigenous peoples and ethnic minority groups on such decision-making bodies accords with the democratic principle of recognising particular communities of interest as well as the specific needs of disadvantaged or marginalised social groups. To achieve this social objective in education there should be a threshold number of ethnic minority and indigenous representatives on such bodies to ensure that their views and interests are effectively expressed. Of course, it is *not* the case that only members of such groups can understand or represent their interests; clearly there are many Anglo-Australians who are engaged in the ongoing struggles against racism and the threat it poses to democracy. However such understanding and representation is not possible without the presence of any ethnic minority or indigenous members. Further, without a threshold number of indigenous and ethnic minority repre-sentatives, other educational decision-makers will not be in a position to understand, let alone learn how to represent, the interests of these groups. Students could explore the possibilities for creating public spaces in which marginalised social groups such as Australians of Aboriginal and Asian background can legitimise their identities as part of democratically inspired attempts by them to take control of their own lives. This is likely to encourage them to take part in society's democratic processes as citizens rather than as consumers.

Supporting the sociocultural conditions for freedom

Second, within this perspective on the nation which is attentive to the politics of difference it is important to support the sociocultural conditions people need to exercise freedom. That is to say, it is important for us as individuals to be able to make free choices, especially about the issues of real significance to our lives. For example, it is important for us as individuals to be able to form our own views about what constitutes a "good life", and to freely revise our beliefs about these issues. However, there are certain cultural and political preconditions that make real the possibilities for such choices. For example, there have to be conditions that make people aware of different views about the "good life", such as education, freedom of expression and freedom of association. Our cultural resources not only provide us with options from which we can freely choose and help us to give meaning to our choices but give reality to one significant perspective on nation — democracy. The cultural resources of democracy include anti-racist education, the freedom to express one's ideas in one's first language, and the freedom to form associations among people having a shared interest in a particular ethnic or indigenous culture. Because people's capacity to make meaningful choices depends on their access to their cultural resources, ethnic minority and indigenous students need access to their own cultural structures. Thus, indigenous and ethnic minority rights to have a culturally responsive education, to freely express themselves in community languages, and to freely associate with kith and kin, are consistent with and help to advance individual freedom, because the exercising of these rights is intimately connected to their cultures. In so far as ethnic minority and indigenous cultures provide students with options that are meaningful to them, they make an important and necessary contribution to individual freedom.

Teachers frequently seek to address the issue of how to ensure that schools are hospitable to indigenous and ethnic minority students and to the politics surrounding their expression of their ethnic or indigenous differences. Their aim is to make indigenousness and ethnicity acceptable and normal features of school life just as they are normal features of life in Australia's multicultural society. And yet education systems need to play a greater role in helping Australian society meet its responsibility — its obligation — to ensure international justice, by challenging the vilification of Australians of Asian and Aboriginal backgrounds, confronting attacks on the democratic rights of indigenous and ethnic minority groups, and ensuring the redistribution of educational resources to meet the needs of all poor students. To enable the successful integration of indigenous and ethnic minority students into schools, and into Australia's multicultural society generally, there is a need for strong efforts by education systems to combat racism, prejudice and discrimination, efforts that need to be supported by the rigorous enforcement of anti-discrimination laws and changes in the portrayal of ethnic minorities and indigenous peoples in school textbooks, government documents and the media. For instance, the goal of ensuring that ethnic minorities learn standardised English as their second language is more likely to be enhanced if they are encouraged to maintain and use their first language (Rockhill and Tomic 1995: 209-229). The aim of education authorities, then, should be to produce students who are fluent bilinguals. This means that ethnic minority students would be able to maintain and develop their heritage, that society would have access to a valuable resource in the context of global restructuring, and that the productive integration of ethnic minorities into Australia's multicultural society would be achieved. Moreover, bilingual education may help to undercut the heritage of racist antagonism towards ethnic minority languages.

Eliminating disadvantages and alleviating vulnerability

A nation which is attentive to the politics of ethnic and indigenous difference would address a third important issue, namely the elimination of the disadvantages and the alleviation of the vulnerabilities confronting indigenous and ethnic minority students. Government decisions on the languages to be taught, the public holidays to be celebrated and the national symbols (flags, songs, anthems, awards) to be honoured in schools involve recognising, accommodating or otherwise supporting the needs and identities of particular ethnic groups, typically some elite fragment of the dominant ethnic group. For instance, the government has decided that standardised English is the language of public schooling. In making this decision, it has provided a very significant support for certain societal cultures, guaranteeing:

> the passing on of the language and its associated traditions and conventions to the next generation. Refusing to provide public schooling in a minority language, by contrast, is almost inevitably condemning that language to ever-increasing marginalization. (Kymlicka 1995: 111)

Governments cannot avoid supporting certain societal cultures; thus, if it supports the ethnic majority language in schools, it should also officially recognise and support ethnic minority and indigenous languages. Because there is no way for the state to avoid supporting one or other ethnic group, it has to decide on a fair way of recognising and attending to society's diverse languages and cultures. Different provisions have to be made to eliminate structural disadvantage and to alleviate vulnerabilities such as racial hatred and its consequences. Therefore, because government is necessarily engaged in the promotion of certain ethnic identities, it needs to ensure that it does not disadvantage others. To do so governments must recognise that ethnic and indigenous minorities must not be left at a social disadvantage in these areas.

Democratic rights for indigenous and ethnic minority groups are socially just where they seek to eliminate these disadvantages, and where they alleviate these groups from vulnerabilities to external forces of oppression.

Discriminatory policies, due to indifference towards the structural disadvantages and vulnerabilities of ethnic and indigenous minorities, relegate them to the margins of society. Antagonism to their democratic rights as minorities is inconsistent with the obligation of democratic nations to protect the interests of minority groups. Having a school-week that was established to favour Christians, then it is fair for schools to have exemptions which redress disadvantages faced by students of other religious faiths (eg, Muslim-Australians, Jewish-Australians). Likewise, a school dress code that suits students from the majority ethnic group, that does not conflict with its beliefs and needs, means that exemptions should be made for students from ethnic minority groups (eg, Sikh-Australians, Orthodox Jewish-Australians). Australian national symbols – the head of government, flags, anthem and song – reflect and privilege a particular ethnic background. The demand by indigenous and ethnic minority groups for some symbolic affirmation of the value of their presence is simply a demand that their identity be given similar recognition to that of the English. What, then, are some of the important social objectives for education in a democratic nation that acknowledges both the multicultural and multi-racist features of its society?

Social objectives for education

The social objectives for education in multicultural and multi-racist Australia reflect one perspective on the idea of nation, namely that a democracy is attentive to the politics of ethnic and indigenous differences. The educational commitments and societal vision listed below are intended to be benchmarks or indicators of the commitment and desire among indigenous and ethnic minority groups to contribute to Australian society. The promotion of their integration into a multicultural and anti-racist society is likely to be enhanced if their cultural differences are protected. These benchmarks reflect the fact that their underlying demands are for visible participation and recognisable integration into Australia's multicultural society, and are in no way a rejection of it:

1. **Educational decision-making must be seen to be inclusive of ethnic minorities and indigenous peoples.** By and large decision-making processes in education authorities have been

60

unrepresentative, failing to reflect the ethnic diversity of the Australian population. The demand for representation rights by indigenous and ethnic minority groups is a demand for inclusion; recognition and accommodation of their "differences" facilitates this. Such representation of these groups promotes civic participation and legitimises the educational system.

2. **Public funding is provided to support the educative practices of indigenous peoples and ethnic minorities** (eg, magazines, festivals, arts, languages, museums) so as to preserve and develop the wealth of Australia's diverse cultural resources, and to ensure that these groups are not discriminated against.

3. **Indigenous peoples and ethnic minorities are able to freely express their ethnicity *as a product of Australian society*, and to do so without fear of prejudice or discrimination.** Schools can help ethnic and indigenous minorities express their particular cultural differences with pride while furthering their successful participation in Australian society. The virtues of having a diversity of such groups within multicultural Australia are that it contributes to the richness of the lives of all Australians; it expands the cultural resources available to create a more interesting society; and it increases the range of choices available to all Australians.

4. **Positive steps are taken to combat discrimination and prejudice in and through schools.** Such racist hostility is, at present, particularly noticeable against Australians of indigenous and Asian backgrounds. Anti-migrant prejudice, racism and xenophobia often lead to the failure to see the desire among ethnic minorities and indigenous peoples for solidarity, and the wish to form coalitions.

5. **Cultural imperialism in the school curriculum is challenged**, so that the stereotyping and invisibility of indigenous peoples and ethnic minorities is changed.

6. **Educational regulations, rules or codes do not disadvantage or reduce the cultural viability of ethnic minority or indigenous students because of their ethno-religious practices** (eg, wearing the turban, yarmulke or chador). It is recognised that the existing educational order privileges students of Anglo-

Christian backgrounds, for instance through the language of schooling and the choice of public holy days.

7. **Indigenous peoples and ethnic minority students have a legally guaranteed and financially secure right to a culturally responsive education.** Justice and freedom in a democratic society require that the interests of the relatively powerless be protected from the relatively powerful.

8. **Indigenous and ethnic minority students are protected from such pressures as hate speech, racism, and group libel.** Schools and education authorities endorse the protection of inter-group relations through specifically designated rights aimed to promote fairness between groups. Efforts are made to redress vulnerabilities and to rectify disadvantages between indigenous/ethnic minority and majority groups.

9. **Schools reject restrictions which limit the rights of students from indigenous and ethnic minority backgrounds.** By and large ethnic minority and indigenous groups are not concerned with imposing internal restrictions on their members. There is freedom *within* all ethnic groups in order to protect civil and political liberties; freedom to question and, if desired, revise community practices; and freedom to choose whether they maintain their ethnic identity.

10. **Conflict in schools is resolved by good-faith negotiations and fairness in procedures, definitions and interpretations.** The interests, needs and perspectives of ethnic minority and indigenous students are listened to, heard and taken into account given the racist culture present in Australian society.

11. **Schools support the hyphenated identity of their students, enabling them to assert pride in both their Australianness and *the ways in which their ethnicity constitutes such Australianness.*** A common identity that is open to ethnic differences provides an important basis for an over-arching societal bond. National identity and difference are symbiotic because people's identities, loyalties and obligations are always and necessarily multiple and multi-layered, rather than existing in a one-dimensional relationship to a racialised nation-state. The idea and practice of Australianness in schools is to be no longer restricted to mean Australians of English ethnic descent.

12. **Ethnic minorities are known in schools by their best features**, by those attributes which are a source of pride, rather than forever being constructed as a "problem" by governments, media and politicians. Also, it is a mistake to assume that ethnic minorities can be solely known through their experiences of social injustice.

How can educators who are committed to a perspective on an Australian nation that is based on these benchmarks of a democratic society seek to achieve these social objectives?

Assuring the achievement of social objectives

There is no one best practice that can be used to assure us that we are achieving these important social objectives for education in a multicultural and multi-racist society. Attempts to reform education by applying what is held to be the "one best solution" seem to ignore the inadequacies and contradictions that emerge in practice. Given that the pursuit of these social objectives will meet opposition and will be used to advance goals other than those proposed here there is a need to accept the vulnerability of all strategies that tell us the one best way these objectives might be achieved. Strategically, it is not desirable to think that there is a single approach to achieving these objectives; this can be self-defeating. On the contrary, teachers attracted to these objectives need an array of strategies for them to test, stretch, critique and elaborate upon under the particular political conditions of their schools. This section provides an overview of several options which may be used to guide and indicate the tentative "achievement" of these objectives, but given the open-ended and generative capacity of both education and democracy, there will be the inevitable supplementation of what has been proposed here. The efforts to organise the curriculum need to start with the interests of indigenous and ethnic minorities (along with other socially marginalised groups), creating a new knowledge-base in the process of curriculum and pedagogical change. Thus, the idea that this knowledge is merely an inadvertent appendage of the existing curriculum needs to be rejected.

From history to histories

There is now a need for a curriculum which acknowledges the differing interpretations of Australia's past. This is as necessary for the continuing development of multicultural democracy as it is to free all Australians from the constraints of historical ignorance. If teachers and students are coerced into ignoring or forgetting about one of these aspects of

Australia's multi-dimensional history, they will be distorting all of our history. Besides, what could be more patriotic than for Australians of indigenous or Asian background to ask how their knowledge, experiences and histories can be best represented in the curriculum? Through continuing re-examination of the strengths and weaknesses of curriculum accounts of Australian society, its histories and traditions, schools play their part in revitalising democracy. In this way schools may be able to engage students in a dialogue intended to renew their interest in democracy and engage them as citizens.

The history of our multicultural society should be studied using a contrapuntal rather than univocal approach, with a simultaneous engagement with both dominant accounts and those other histories against which the dominant history acts (Said 1993: 59). There is the history of Aboriginal Australia and its relations with Asia, Europe and other parts of the world; the feminist history of Aboriginal women, and the history of Aboriginal workers. Then there is the history of the British empire with its expansionism, divide-and-rule strategies, and its treatment of the Aboriginal, Islander and Asian peoples it colonised. It is also important that Anglo-Celtic students are able to recover and interrogate their ethnic experiences and histories; there is need for histories of the British Isles which take students beyond the pageantry of royalty. Here there might be room for a history of Australia that challenges the story of the origins of western European culture in ancient Greece, recognising that Greek culture was dependent upon and derived from African and Asian cultures (Bernal 1991). There is also the history of Australia as a nation state, formed through the consolidation of the British colonies which had come to dominate this continent, and a nationalist ideology that upheld the culture of the majority ethnic group — or at least its masculinist element — in opposition to and despite the strong indigenous, South Sea Islander and Asian presence. It made no commitment to the survival of ethnic minority or indigenous cultures, on the contrary it set out to destroy such cultures, for instance through taking Aboriginal children from their parents, and to exclude the peoples of Asia and the Pacific Ocean regions. Ironically, to assert that Australia is a European nation is not only to remind us of the officially institutionalised anti-Asian, anti-Pacific Islander, anti-Aboriginal racisms expressed in the "White Australia" policy which was used to enforce Anglo-ethnic hegemony in Australia for 50 years of its 200-year history, but to incite the reassertion of this policy and its associated racist practices. Another history concerns contemporary Australia as a postcolonial, diasporic society and seeks to provide an answer to such questions as: "Why have Asian students, tourists, business people and migrants become a significant feature of Australian society and its changing global relations? What has made it possible for indigenous peoples to overturn the claim that at the time of British colonisation Australia was a land without people?"

Engaging in dialogic education

One approach to education for a multicultural society is to give students experiences in negotiating shared values through "dialogic education". Schools can practice democracy in a way that includes but goes beyond reading the Australian Constitution and learning about the roles of the Federal, State and local governments. Multicultural democracy involves learning to articulate the socioeconomic and cultural interests of one's own ethnic minority or indigenous community; learning how to debate culturally, economically and socially significant issues, and learning to create the conditions for such debates; organising and working collectively with fellow citizens on community action projects; and knowing how to acquire and exercise power. Students from indigenous and ethnic minority groups must:

> develop a sense of political efficacy, and be given practice in ... strategies of active citizenship which teaches them how to get power without violence and further exclusion ... Opportunities for [informed and active citizenship], in which students have experience in obtaining and exercising power should be emphasized within a curriculum that is designed to help liberate excluded ethnic [minority and indigenous] groups. (Banks in Sleeter and Grant 1988: 187)

The social objectives of education in a multicultural and multi-racist society are not just concerned about differences, but require the ongoing development and redevelopment of shared values. Commonalities in values could be extended, so that shared values in one domain can provide a balance against conflicts elsewhere. Disagreements over significant social, cultural and economic issues are important in educating students for/about democratic multiculturalism and against racism, sexism and class exploitation. Of course, we are all too conscious of those who are keen to subjugate or otherwise exclude ethnic minorities and indigenous peoples, rather than engage them in dialogic education. The pitting of some imaginary "us" against a demonised "them" makes it impossible to negotiate cultural understandings through the work of educating for a multicultural and non-racist society. By bringing various indigenous and ethnic groups together to engage in dialogue, students and teachers can explore possibilities for community interaction; for enriching Australia's cultural diversity; and for creating a new consensus about the common wealth we have in our diverse cultural heritage. Dialogic education seeks to build bridges that connect the concerns of one group of Australians with those of another, and seeks to build points of commonality among different groups of people.

Analysing the situation of one's own group

Schools can help indigenous and ethnic minority students, among others, to analyse their own group's life situation; to develop their knowledge of the social injustices in society which affect their group; and to consider the constructive responses made by their group and supporters of their struggles for a nation attentive to the politics of difference. This work might usefully be approached by helping students to learn to read and write using words that will help them examine the constraints on giving expression to the democratic virtues in their own people's lives. They need to read texts that relate to the realities of their group's life situation. Students could also be taught how to critically analyse and question texts in terms of the social interests they serve. The curriculum should not be silent about the social injustices associated with racism, patriarchy and poverty. On the contrary, it could help students examine issues of power-lessness, exploitation, marginalisation, cultural imperialism, violence and exploitation (Young 1990), as well as ways in which these reproduce the subordination of the least advantaged and the marginalised in society. Similarly, the curriculum could help students from indigenous and ethnic minority backgrounds to analyse the impact of current immigration legislation and anti-migrant campaigns against their communities and themselves. They should carefully examine the evidence regarding the claim that migrants are taking the jobs of white Anglo-Australians against evidence regarding other possible explanations for the disappearance of jobs, such as the role of "labour saving" technology:

Ask the printers, postal workers, bank tellers, telephone operators, office workers, grocery clerks, airline reservation agents, warehouse workers, autoworkers, steelworkers, dockworkers – if you can find them. Computer-aided manufacturing, robotics, computer inventories, automated switchboards and tellers, telecommunications technologies – all have been used to displace and replace people, to enable employers to reduce labour costs, contract-out, relocate operations. From the factory to the farm, from the oil refinery to the office, no workplace has been immune to this assault. (Noble 1995: xii-xiii)

Developing citizen action competencies

The development of students' citizen action competencies is an opportunity to link their democratic skills, knowledge and understandings with issues involving racism, sexism and poverty in their everyday life. Citizen action competencies may be thought of as the knowledge, attitudes and skills needed by informed and active citizens in a democracy to help realise economic, cultural and social improvements in their society. Students from some groups, including indigenous and ethnic minority groups, may not have the competencies to secure, maintain, and efficaciously use power. Where this is so, it is important that this goal not be neglected in education, otherwise it renders hollow Australia's claim to be a participatory democracy. Given that schools are connected with various indigenous institutions and ethnic community organisations in Australian society, it is important that they work with them so as not to reinforce inequality but to investigate possibilities for socially just changes. Of course, schools do not operate independently of the contradictory forces at work in Australian society, but they can still play a significant role in advancing traditional Australian values of egalitarianism and a fair go. Schools can and should reflect in the curriculum their vision of the virtues of democracy, among which freedom, power sharing and social justice must rate highly.

Building cross-sectoral support

Democratic education seeks to promote coalescence across groups which have been variously disadvantaged and marginalised by inappropriate and inadequate responses to their class location, ethnic formation or gender relations. There are several good reasons why students from indigenous and ethnic minority groups should learn about the formation of coalitions and the creation of cross-sectional cross-sectoral support. First, the issues of racism, poverty and sexism are not separate issues; rather they merge with one another, often in contradictory ways (McCarthy 1990). Of course, they each raise similar concerns about power relations, freedom and social justice. Perhaps, more significantly, it is important to recognise that all people are variously positioned, structurally and subjectively, by their gender, ethnicity and social class. A further reason for learning to form cross-sectoral support, is that the coalescing of variously disadvantaged or otherwise marginalised groups, with those in solidarity with their struggles for democracy, makes for a powerful majority. For example, while indigenous people may have a relatively weak power base numerically, they gain considerable strength when joined by Australians of Asian background, and much additional strength if joined by Anglo-Australians, feminists and environmentalists among others. Marginalised and relatively powerless groups can waste their time fighting among themselves over ever-decreasing "handouts", or alternatively they can learn to work together, recognising the commonalities and significant differences in their agendas (Knowles and Mercer 1992), so as to achieve a more just, rational and amicable society.

Conclusion

The social objectives for education outlined in this chapter are consistent with Australia's democratic principles on power relations, freedom and justice. Moreover, they provide a good opportunity to contribute to a stable society wherein there is mutual accommodation of cultural differences; a shared concern for those of ethnically different backgrounds, and a willingness to make sacrifices on behalf of others. The strengthening of the affiliation of indigenous and ethnic minority groups to Australian society requires much more than the ambivalent assertion of racial toleration by parliament; it requires governments and education authorities to explicitly and officially sanction cultural difference as an expression of Australianness along with the accommodation and recognition of such difference in schools. Such allegiance is possible through schools where people's ethnic identity is nurtured, rather than subordinated or marginalised. Schools need to give due recognition to the fact that not only do Australians come from different ethnic backgrounds, they also have different ways in which they express their sense of belonging, their sense of Australianness.

References

Anthias, F. and N. Yuval-Davis (1992) *Racialized Boundaries: Race, Nation, Gender, Colour and Class and Anti-racist Struggle*. London: Routledge.

Bernal, M. (1991) *Black Athena: The AfroAsiatic Roots of Classical Civilization: vol 1: The Fabrication of Ancient Greece 1785-1985*. London: Vintage Books.

Bhabha, H. (ed) (1990) *Nation and Narration*. London: Routledge.

Bottomley, G., M. de Lepervanche and J. Martin (eds) (1991) *Intersexions: Gender/Class/Culture/Ethnicity.* Sydney: Allen and Unwin.

Brandt, G.L. (1986) *The Realization of Anti-racist Teaching.* London: Falmer.

Buell, F. (1994) *National Culture and the New Global System.* Baltimore: Johns Hopkins University Press.

Castles, S., B. Cope, M. Kalantzis and M. Morrissey (1988) *Mistaken Identity: Multiculturalism and the Demise of Nationalism in Australia.* Sydney: Pluto Press.

Donald, J and A. Rattansi (eds) (1992) *"Race", Culture and Difference.* London: Sage.

Gilroy, P (1987) *There Ain't No Black in the Union Jack: The Cultural Politics of Race and Nation.* London: Hutchinson.

Goldberg, D.L. (1994) *Multiculturalism: A Critical Reader.* Oxford: Blackwell.

Guillory, J. (1993) *Cultural Capital: The Problem of Literary Canon Formation.* Chicago: University of Chicago Press.

Gunew, S. and F. Rizvi (ed) (1994) *Culture, Difference and the Arts.* Sydney: Allen and Unwin.

Gunew, S. and A. Yeatman (eds) (1993) *Feminism and the Politics of Difference.* Sydney: Allen and Unwin.

Habermas, J. (1971) *Toward a Rational Society.* London: Heinemann.

hooks, b (1990) *Yearning: Race, Gender and Cultural Politics.* Boston: South End Press.

hooks, b (1994) *Teaching to Transgress: Education as the Practice of Freedom.* New York: Routledge.

Jakubowicz, A. (ed) (1994) *Racism, Ethnicity and the Media.* Sydney: Allen and Unwin.

Kanpol, B. and P. McLaren (1995) *Critical Multiculturalism: Uncommon Voices in a Common Struggle.* Westport, Connecticut: Bergin and Garvey.

Knowles, C and S. Mercer (1992) "Feminism and Antiracism: An Exploration of the Political Possibilities" in J. Donald and A. Rattansi (eds) *"Race", Culture and Difference.* London: Sage.

Kymlicka, W. (1995) *Multicultural Citizenship: A Liberal Theory of Minority Rights.* Oxford: Oxford University Press.

Luke, A. (1988) *Literacy, Textbooks and Ideology: Postwar Literacy Instruction and the Mythology of Dick and Jane.* London: Falmer.

McCarthy, C. and W. Crichlow (1993) *Race, Identity and Representation in Education.* New York: Routledge.

McCarthy, C. (1990) *Race and Curriculum: Social Inequality and the Theories and Politics of Difference in Contemporary Research on Schooling*. London: Falmer.

Miles, R. (1989) *Racism*. London: Routledge.

Modood, T. (1992) *Not Easy Being British: Colour, Culture and Citizenship*. Stoke-on-Trent: Trentham Books.

Norman, R. (1987) *Free and Equal*. Oxford: Oxford University Press.

Mohanty, C., A. Russo and L. Torres (eds) (1991) *Third World Women and the Politics of Feminism*. Bloomington: Indiana University Press.

Noble, D. (1995) *Progress Without People: New Technology, Unemployment and the Message of Resistance*. Toronto: Between the Lines.

Omi, M. and H. Winant (1986) *Racial Formation in the United States: From the 1960s to the 1980s*. New York: Routledge.

Rattansi, A. and S. Westwood (eds) (1994) *Racism, Modernity and Identity: On the Western Front*. Cambridge: Polity Press.

Rockhill, K. and P. Tomic (1995) "Situating ESL Between Speech and Silence" in J. Gaskell and J. Willinsky (eds) *Gender In/forms Curriculum: From Enrichment to Transformation*. New York: Teachers College Press, pp 209-229.

Said, E. (1993) *Culture and Imperialism*. London: Chatto and Windus.

Tomlinson, S. (1990) *Multicultural Education in White Schools*. London: Batsford.

Vasta, E. and S. Castles (eds) (1995) *The Teeth Are Smiling: The Persistence of Racism in Multicultural Australia*. Sydney: Allen and Unwin.

Viswanathan, G. (1995) "The Beginnings of English Literary Study in India" in B. Ashcroft, G. Griffiths and H. Tiffin (eds) *The Post-colonial Studies Reader*. London: Routledge.

West, C. (1993) *Race Matters*. Boston: Beacon Press.

Young, I.M. (1990) *Justice and the Politics of Difference*. Princeton: Princeton University Press.

5

Re-tooling schooling?

Information technology, cultural change, and the future(s) of Australian education

Bill Green and Chris Bigum

What might be an appropriate educational response to the emerging forms of information technology? More broadly: How does education contribute to the shaping and indeed the definition of Australian culture? These are the questions that we seek here to engage and explore, in contemplating the challenges and changes confronting schools and the Australian community in these last few years of the transition to the 21st century. Figuring centrally in this is *information technology* – the "new technologies", more specifically those associated with text, image, information and communication, the "digital revolution" or, simply, "computing". As we shall indicate, these are far from settled or agreed-upon formulations. The phenomenon at issue here – in effect, a question of widespread social and cultural change – is both particularly complex and much contested, and subject therefore to extensive and ongoing debate and disputation.

This chapter will address the relationship between education, information technology and cultural practice, with specific reference to new and emerging problematics and realisations of technology, information and communication, and changing forms of and imperatives in Australian society. Its organising assumption is that Australia is fast becoming a distinctively postmodern society, uniquely positioned both geo-politically and socioculturally, and poised to enter decisively into a new, post-capitalist Information Age. This runs counter to much current discussion of these matters, which tends to work with the understanding that Australia is already in such an era and such a phase. Our own position in this regard is that Australia is in transition – although it may be that to be in this new digitised era is to be *always* "in transition". New developments in technoscience and information technology, and its associated infrastructure and forms of complementarity, will be critical in successfully negotiating this transition and in moving productively and pro-actively into a dynamic, creative future.

An important aspect of this is the increasing emphasis on and investment in the relationship between information technology and educational change. Since the late 1970s, when the first microcomputers appeared, Australian schools have been working to come to terms with the new information and communication technologies. What began as a hobbyist interest in the then new microcomputer technology, involving a handful of teachers, has over a relatively short time become an "essential" component of most classrooms. Moreover, for secondary schools in particular, it now occupies a significant proportion of curriculum time, space and teaching resources (Bigum 1990). During the last 15 years, schools and school systems have become sufficiently persuaded of the importance of computers in classrooms that their educational response has been to make significant and ongoing expenditure in computer hardware, software and support. The investment in computer technology supported by policy makers, administrators and teachers is consistent with a widely held discourse which associates computers in classrooms with technological progress, improved future employment opportunities of students, and enhanced learning in the classroom (Iacono and Kling 1996; see also Bigum and Green 1993a).

Making an educational response to the new information and communication technologies is not as obvious as might first appear, therefore. In the early 1980s, the educational merits of computers in classrooms were yet to be established. Schools acquired modest numbers of the first eight-bit microcomputers, such as the Apple IIe, TRS80 and Commodore 64. Acquisition of more computers and the replacement or upgrading of out-of-date machines continued apace, while teachers worked hard to establish an educational legitimacy and so make this an educational technology *for the classroom* (Bigum et al 1987). This involved unpaid product development engineering (Franklin 1990), something that teachers have carried out since the early 1980s and which continues to be a key element in the way schools respond to the new information and communication technologies. In creating a new *resource* for schooling, however, these teachers have also contributed to constructing a technologically-textured *context* for further acquisition and meaning-making, one that is decidedly "non-neutral" (Idhe 1990).[5]

In the 1990s, we can now see the consequences of a feedback loop operating between rhetoric and reality, context and resource. Many schools now feature networks of computers, and some schools have adopted policies which require all students to own a laptop computer. This is clearly something that is expensive, and an extra pressure on already constrained budgetary resources. As schools continue to improve and add to their computing resources, Becker (1996) has estimated that to properly equip a school with computer technology, and support teachers in their use, costs an additional $2,000 per pupil, per year.[6] The investments that schools have made and are likely to continue to make are clearly substantial. Apart from diverting resources from other areas of the curriculum, the growing use of computers in schools contributes significantly to producing an educational legitimacy for computer technology that it otherwise would not have. Regardless of what they are used for in classrooms, however, computers are now firmly linked to public perceptions of modern educational practice, and their growing use in the home appears to be linked to a now general acceptance of their educational worth.

Growing social acceptance of computer technology, coupled to widespread commercial promotion of the educational value of computer technology, has meant a significant rise in the ownership of computers in the homes of school-age children, particularly those in secondary schools.[7] Increasing numbers of teachers now report students negotiating to do their computer-based work at home, because they have better access to better hardware and software there. However, the change in home ownership of computers is only one of a number of changes associated with the growing use of computers that have taken place *outside* schools (Bigum et al 1994) since the early 1980s. Importantly, the world in which schools first began to use computers is itself much changed, largely due to increasing computerisation and global computer networks (Sassen 1991; Castells 1991). Notwithstanding this, schools and school systems have with some notable exceptions continued to respond to computer

---

5   On the relationship between *context* and *resource*, see Bigum and Green (1995).

6   The assumptions in Becker's model translate well for Australia.

7   Surveys of urban schools in Victoria indicate 90 to 95 per cent computer ownership in the home for students in the upper years of secondary schools.

technology in much the same way as they always have (Bigum 1995b), acting in accord with a rather narrow and limited view not only of the role of computer technology in education and in the world more generally (Kenway 1996), but also of the very nature and significance of technocultural change and development in postmodern societies.

In an era in which government expenditure on education is declining (Kenway et al 1995) and yet the promotion of the new information and communication technologies continues apace (Kenway 1995), schools are finding it increasingly difficult to finance the acquisition of contemporary computer technology. The commitment of most schools to a rhetoric of technological progress locates them in a broad social movement that supports computer-based education (Iacono and Kling 1996). Their engagement with technoculture (Penley and Ross 1991) is characterised, however, more by consumption and the imperatives of image and impression-management predicated on "high tech savvy" than with providing appropriate experiences so as to produce a citizenry capable of making informed choices about the new information and communication technologies, *and* the social forms they cultivate and support.

Some argue that they have little choice in this regard, given the increasing competition for students between schools and the need to have at least a gloss of "high tech" to show parents. Although reluctant to admit it, then, schools are clearly caught in an increasingly expensive pattern of consumption of high-technology products. We believe that schools can no longer continue to operate in this way, however, and that they would be better able to adapt to changed and changing technosocial conditions if they engaged a more pluralistic view of computers and related technologies in classrooms, thereby adopting a broader view of their engagements with computers and related technologies.

In what follows, we elaborate firstly on questions of culture, context and vision, with specific reference to the relationship between education and information technology, and secondly on strategies for realising such a (re)visionary account of schooling, in terms of a critical assessment of the future(s) of Australian education.

1

Of particular importance in this respect is the development of an adequate, energising social and educational *vision* – an informed sense of possibility. This is directly related to the question of "the future", and therefore of the prospects as they stand currently for Australian culture, education, society and community. This matter is, of course, best understood with specific reference to history and tradition, and to the changing "story" of Australia as it is both re-told and renewed in and through the curriculum, through schooling and other educational practices and forms. But it also means taking a good hard look at the present moment in that history, without sentiment or nostalgia. Out of this is likely to emerge a powerful, intensely specific *and* grounded sense of crisis and change, as it now being lived through, in the everyday life and work of countless Australians, as well as in traditional, mainstream forms of education and schooling.

Our starting point is the significance of information technology in this regard, and of technoscientific development more generally. There is widespread consensus on this point. A representative statement here is the group of scenarios developed by CSIRO, addressed to forecasting the nature of Australian society in 2020 (Eckersley and Jeans 1995). A key role is assigned to science and technology, as "the most powerful forces shaping our destiny" (Stocker and Eckersley 1995: 4). They cite leading strategist and futurist Peter Schwartz to this effect: "The single most frequent failure in the history of forecasting has been grossly under-estimating the impact of technologies", and observe that "[t]he reason we under-estimate the impacts of science and technology is that they are so difficult, if not impossible, to forsee" (Stocker and Eckersley 1995: 5). As they write:

> we face a conundrum in thinking about the future. Science and technology are the main forces for change in the modern world. Yet their impacts are highly uncertain, even impossible to anticipate. (Stocker and Eckersley 1995: 6)

This makes forecasting a business fraught with hazard, with risk and uncertainty. Any contemplation of "futures" must therefore be conjectural, and always already provisional – especially those articulated in one way or another with technological change and development.

Commentators such as Ian Lowe (1992) and Barry Jones (1990) are similarly insistent on the role and significance of technology in this regard. As Lowe (1992: 48) writes:

> We are currently in the middle of a technological revolution which is changing society every bit as fundamentally as the Industrial Revolution did. The information technology revolution is permeating every aspect of human behaviour.

He notes also the difficulties in forecasting, stressing that "technological change is a *social process*" (our emphasis), with clear political dimensions and implications. Along with others, he seeks to emphasise the need for *cultural* change – a shift in focus in terms of values, beliefs and meanings, and forms of life. Importantly this goes beyond explicit, articulated, discursive consciousness, in Gidden's (1984) sense, to embrace the practical and unconscious dimensions of knowledge and awareness – a matter, that is, of "reculturing the future", as Sharan Burrows (1994) has expressed it, but in such a way as to work for and towards deep-seated change in the ways we live and learn *now*, in both the practice and the very forms of our being and becoming.

Crucially, this involves thinking in terms of fundamental, paradigmatic change, a decisive shift in terms of "frame" or "paradigm", so that human action and meaning can thereby be *recontextualised*. Arguably we are poised at such a moment. Beare and Slaughter (1993) are among a growing body of educationists who are turning their attention to these issues, challenges and questions, albeit against the grain of official or established forms of educational theory and practice. "Most of the writing, planning and public debate about education", they write (1993: 4), assumes a fairly static world-picture. Schools, students, the curriculum, classrooms, teachers, and the policies and functions of educational systems are treated as if they have been, are, and will continue to be enduring features of education, wherever we are in the world.

This is clearly no longer tenable, if indeed it ever was. The world *is* changing, inexorably, and so too must education. Moreover, we live in a time of decisive and dynamic change – when change is, as Giddens (1984: 199) puts it, "white hot" – and educators must respond accordingly, and as much as possible positively and pro-actively. Yet the signs are not all that promising in this regard. Beare and Slaughter (1993: 7) observe the following:

> We are . . . at a major historical divide. Many writers and commentators have been making this point for several decades. This transition away from what we have taken for granted affects the viability of all institutions and the life of every individual. Yet, curiously, there is little evidence that those running schools are aware of these rapid, fundamental, and structural changes.

Hence, as they indicate, the current dilemmas and problems in education "have no lasting or satisfactory solutions while schools operate out of the framework that has determined their *raison d'etre* for the past two hundred years".[8] More radical, *interruptive* thinking is required: "Education does not need fine-tuning, or more of the same; rather the fundamental assumptions about schooling have to be revised" (Beare and Slaughter 1993: 1).

Among a range of such commentary, Stocker and Eckersley (1995) note that there is widespread concern about the very notion of "*a* future", and of futures generally, especially among the young. As they write:

> Many young people believe the world is out of control – "going down the gurgler", as one report put it. Numerous surveys over the past ten years reveal this pessimism. They suggest a deepening concern about war, global environmental destruction, growing violence and inequality, chronic high unemployment and an increasingly dehumanised, machine-dominated world. (Stocker and Eckersley 1995: 3)

While such a pessimistic image of young people might well be contested, or understood rather as a *construction*, nonetheless there would indeed seem to be a widespread loss of faith and growing disillusion and disaffection among many young people today (Green and Bigum 1993; Bigum, Fitzclarence and Green 1994; Fitzclarence, Green and Bigum 1995). Importantly, Stocker and Eckersley (1995: 4) see this "lack of faith in the future" as "a cultural failing – the lack of an appealing and coherent vision of who we are and where we are going". In broad terms, this is a point similarly emphasised by Lowe (1992: 51) and also by Beare and Slaughter (1993: 14-15).[9]

What this suggests in this context is the crucial role and significance of notions of *culture* and *imagination*. How to both inform and inspire people, especially young people – the constituency of schooling, and our future citizenry – is therefore an urgent matter with particular implications for education, at all levels, but perhaps especially that of schooling. Developing an adequate social and educational vision, *and*

---

8   A point to bear in mind here is how to account critically for more "futuristic" *bureaucratic* initiatives in this regard – for example, the "Classrooms of the Future" policy in Victoria.

9   Although to what extent views such as these are fully representative of young people's lives, and their own sense of their world, might well be debated.

77

making it both worldly and meaningful, is a major challenge.[10] It requires that cultural change becomes a focus point for debate and praxis. As Stocker and Eckersley (1995: 4) write:

> We need a positive vision to engage people, especially our youth – to convince them there is something beyond themselves to believe in and live for. This is a vital function of culture.

Moreover, this involves the creative intersection of new and emerging forms of education and information technology, within a rich technoscientific *culture*. This is something central to the former Labor Federal government's cultural policy statement ("Creative Nation"), and is likely to similarly inform, if more in spirit than formally, the policies of the present Coalition government: "Information technology, and all that it offers, has crossed the technical rubicon into the realm of consciousness, to the realm of culture" (Commonwealth of Australia 1994: 55). Crucially, therefore, systematic attention needs to be given to education, culture and technology as matters of enormous moment and formative power in terms of Australia's future. Above all else, however, this means developing, in Kress's (1995) terms, "a culture of innovation", or an innovative, productive, actively *designing* and *imagining*, creative culture. How might this be done, and what does it involve?

A central issue here is reassessing the very idea of the school. This is so much part of our commonsense, our taken-for-granted experience, our very memories, that we run the risk of forgetting that schooling in the forms that we know it today is a relatively recent invention. The coincidence of education with schooling is, in fact, a bounded historical phenomenon, and is thoroughly implicated in the distinctive project of modern(ist), industrial society – something that, as many commentators have argued, may well be either coming to an end or else undergoing major and decisive transformation, so much so that a new social form is emerging and consolidating all around us. Attendant on this are shifts in world-view, or structures of sensibility and intelligibility, across a range

---

10 Whether any *single* vision can operate thus as an "ordering device" might well be debated. As Law (1994: 118) writes: "Visionary orderings don't leave much room for delegation: who can be trusted who is not already graced? The answer is: only those who touch the hem and partake of the state of grace . . . So here's the moral. The orderings of vision tell that there are three states, three levels of possible hierarchy. There is the visionary. There are those that partake indirectly of the vision. And then there are those who do not.

of spheres of human activity, including education. This is the phenomenon of *paradigm shift*. As Beare and Slaughter (1993: 5) note:

> The central importance of changes in values, in ways of knowing, in assumptions about meaning – in short, the implication of paradigm shifts – has too often been overlooked in educational discourse.

Yet, as they further observe, "understanding these deep-seated changes opens up many new options". It is useful, accordingly, to refer more directly at this point to Thomas Kuhn's (1970) account of paradigmatic change and the "structure of scientific revolutions", bearing in mind of course that his focus was on particular areas and aspects of knowledge and praxis. For our purposes here, it is worth noting that his stated aim was "to urge a change in the perception and evaluation of natural data" (Kuhn 1970: ix), which in this case is to be understood in terms of the taken-for-grantedness, or "naturalness", of the idea and the apparatus of the school. How might schooling (as a "natural datum") be reconceptualised, perceived differently, and re-evaluated?[11]

A key image in this respect is that of "re-tooling". As Kuhn (1970: 76) writes:

> As long as the tools a paradigm supplies continue to prove capable of solving the problems it defines, science moves fastest and penetrates more deeply through confident employment of those tools. The reason is clear. As in manufacture so in science – retooling is an extravagance to be reserved for the occasion that demands it. *The significance of crises is the indication they provide that an occasion for retooling has arrived* [our emphasis].

Our argument is that education is currently undergoing just such a "crisis", and that accordingly "an occasion for retooling has arrived", for educational theory and practice alike. There is, moreover, particular resonance in this formulation here, since the metaphor of tools and tooling is directly drawn from accounts and contexts of technology and technological practice, and hence is especially apposite in seeking to assess the educational implications of the new forms of information technology. Our attention is drawn therefore to the matter of *re-tooling schooling*, of seeing how schooling might itself be "re-tooled" in such a way as to allow for a (r)evolution in terms of its organising forms and practices, consistent with larger patterns of societal change.

---

11 An important caveat needs to be made here: It is who *does* this imagining that matters – for instance: economic-rationalist bureaucrats or schools communities? . . .

Such a formulation has the further value of drawing into consideration other debates about educational changes and challenges, notably those associated with the "de-schooling" movement, both in the original terms of Illich's account of the early 1970s (Illich 1971) and in the more recent (revivalist) revisionary terms of "New Age" radical and conservative commentators alike (eg, Papert 1993; Tiffin and Rajasinghan 1995; Hiltz 1994; Lemke 1994; Perelman 1992; see also Bigum and Green 1993a and Bigum and Kenway 1998). The echo of "de-schooling" in the notion of "re-tooling schooling" is quite deliberate, since it is clear that schooling in its received form can no longer be sustained as the sole or hegemonic form of educational practice in and for postmodern conditions. But equally important here is another echo, and another imperative entirely: that of "re-schooling". This refers to the need to re-invent and re-imagine schooling (and the idea of the school), in such a way as to secure its continuing relevance in a new age of technocultural change and complexity. It is precisely in understanding and negotiating this interplay between the respective dynamics and implications of *de*-schooling and *re*-schooling that the challenge is located that confronts us now, in the shadow of a new millennium.

In Kuhnian terms, then, we are confronted with the challenge of "re-tooling schooling" – that is, of recognising that due occasion has arisen now to rethink the nature and the very forms of schooling, as it has been understood for the best part of two centuries. This embraces both how schooling is conceived and how it is practiced, and it includes everything that we commonly associate with schools, such as classrooms, timetables, buildings, textbooks, tests, and "pen-and-paper" (and its equivalents). Added to this are particular roles and personnel, such as those of teacher, student, principal. Part of what is at issue here is understanding how schooling, as a specific institution, might be seen as a distinctive form of "educational technology", a distinctive way of "doing education" or of "getting education done" (Hodas 1996). This is to draw from Franklin's (1990) view of technology as a form of *practice*, which draws in turn on Kenneth Boulding's observation that "there is a technology of prayer as well as of ploughing; there are technologies to control fear as well as to control flood". As Franklin (1990: 15) continues:

> Looking at technology as practice, indeed as formalised practice, has some quite interesting consequences. One is that it links technology directly to culture, because culture, after all, is a set of socially accepted practices and values.

It is in this light that we want to employ the notion of conventional schooling as a form of "educational technology". This immediately raises questions such as: What is education? Or rather: What does education *do*, and what is it *for*? That is, it raises fundamental questions about the *nature* and *purpose* of education, and even its characteristic *look* and *feel*. Furthermore, it provides a way of understanding and engaging the challenges and changes associated with the so-called "new technologies", specifically in their implication for education and schooling. In short, how is *educational* technology changing, particularly and especially in response to new and emerging forms of *information* technology?

Hence, a key aspect of the "re-tooling schooling" idea is the notion of *technologising education* – of bringing digital technologies of various kinds into the normal operation of the school. However, it is also important to understand this as, in a very precise sense, a matter of *re*-technologising the school. This is because the introduction of *digital* technologies – computers and the like – is best understood as overlaying and hence supplementing existing technologies, rather than being something quite new or unprecedented in the experience or the constitution of the school. That is, as well as being a technology in itself (or perhaps a "meta-technology"), schooling always-already draws upon, and is organised in terms of, technologies of various kinds. However, what needs to be recognised here is that, by and large, the "old" technologies have been naturalised and normalised, and taken for granted, to the point where they have become essentially *invisible*.[12]

Noting the consequences of identifying "technology" more or less exclusively with "computers", Bossert (1996: 15) observes that schooling is already heavily technologised, something reflected for instance in its budgetary practices:

> The fact is that most schools do not have funds for [new] technology because they are spending all their money on [old, or existing] technology! – that is, "technology" in the broad sense of the term.

Yet this is still rarely taken into account in much debate on educational change and information technology:

The reason this escapes most of us is that these older technologies have become so much part of our everyday living and learning that we no

---

12 Although patently "essential" – for instance, the various technologies associated with literacy.

longer consider them to be "technologies" at all; they are simply the "environment" within which we live and learn (Bossert 1996: 15).[13]

Particularly important in this regard is the historical role and significance of the printing press (Eisenstein 1979). More broadly, this is a matter bringing together the culture-industries of printing and publishing, and of recognising the role played by what Ulmer (1989: 4) describes as *the print apparatus* with regard to the institution of modern(ist) schooling, and in particular the organic relationship between curriculum and literacy (Green 1993). The very culture of normative schooling is directly connected to the epistemological and organisational effects of the print apparatus – its rational(ist), cognitive emphasis, for instance, its competitive individualism, its rigorous deployment of regularities of speech and silence, its ongoing disciplinary work, or its administrative dynamics of surveillance and control.

Hence what must be accounted for, in this regard, is the notion of a shift from *print* to *digital-electronics* as the organising principle for both schooling and, more broadly, society. This is what has been described variously in terms of "the mode of information" or the "Second Media Age" (Poster 1995), and the "communications revolution" (Hinkson 1991). For high-tech visionary Nicholas Negroponte, what is at issue here is the convergence of the cultures and industries of publishing, broadcasting and computing, increasingly overlaid by the growth and consolidation of global digital networks (Brand 1987; Negroponte 1995). Such lines of argument and technological development have important and even revolutionary implications for education and schooling. This goes well beyond the need for a new emphasis on media literacy and media education, within the curriculum economy of the school, important as these undoubtedly are. Rather, it raises serious questions about the fate and fortunes of schooling itself, at least in its received or familiar form.

Something that must be engaged as a matter of some urgency by educators is the increasing *educational* significance of the media, broadly defined to include multimedia and associated digital technologies. At issue here is a new emphasis on the media as the "dominant ideological

---

13 Except when there is breakdown and hence attention is drawn to these technologies – as in, for instance, current public concerns about literacy, consequent on a socially engineered "literacy crisis".

apparatus", in Althusser's (1971) sense,[14] effectively replacing the school, and redefining in the process not simply relationships among education, state and society but also their very nature. What does this mean for schooling? As we have suggested, rather than looking to *de*-schooling as the inevitable response or consequence, it seems to us extremely important to start thinking creatively and actively about the challenges associated with the idea of *re*-schooling. How might the school be re-imagined in and for new times? What new "tools" do we need for this to happen?

For commentators such as Beare and Slaughter, this means shifting to an informed vision of *the post-industrial school*, modelled on what they described as "the post-bureaucratic organisation" (Beare and Slaughter 1993: 78), which they describe in terms of "constellations" or "networks".[15] Their account is based on an analysis of mass schooling in terms of industrial metaphors such as the "factory". It is worth reiterating here, then, that modern(ist) schooling is a quite recent invention, extending back little more than two centuries. Previous to that, for instance in feudal or so-called pre-historic contexts, education involves very different technologies, of quite different scale and scope. The "school" and the "classroom", in themselves,[16] are exemplary forms of what Deleuze (1992: 3) calls "spaces of enclosure", and as such they represent key technologies in terms of the social logic and practice of what, following Foucault, he describes as "disciplinary societies". As he writes:

> Foucault has brilliantly analyzed the ideal project of these environments of enclosure, particularly visible in the factory: to concentrate; to distribute in space; to order in time; to compose a productive force within the dimension of space-time whose effect will be greater than the sum of its component forces. (Deleuze 1992: 3)

Yet now, and increasingly, "[w]e are in a generalized crisis of all the environments of enclosure – prison, hospital, factory, school, family" (Deleuze 1992: 3-4). This is in accordance with a shift into a new social

---

14 Hinkson (1991) draws upon Althusser in his account of postmodernity, state and education. It needs to be further noted that such arguments need to be recontextualised, and to some extent redrawn, in accordance with the insights and critiques associated with poststructural and postmodern theory.

15 For a more critical assessment of "the high-tech, post-fordist school", see Arnold (1996).

16 And similarly the "textbook" or the "reader" (McHoul 1991).

order, which he calls "the societies of control", understanding this formulation specifically within and in relation to an open semiotic framework, complex in its articulation, with new forms and flows of power and capital. Hence enclosure modulates into openness – a fundamental re-ordering in which enclosure becomes openness (eg, the classroom), or in which what was once seen as openness is turned into new micro forms of enclosure (the home office, the home worker, the home prisoner . . . the home schooler?).

And what does this mean for education? "[J]ust as the corporation replaces the factory, *perpetual training* tends to replace the *school*, and continuous control to replace the examination" – "the surest way", he notes, "of delivering the school over to the corporation". Moreover:

> In the disciplinary societies one was always starting again (from school to the barracks, from the barracks to the factory), while in the societies of control one is never finished with anything – the corporation, the educational system, the armed services being metastable states coexisting in one and the same modulation, like a universal system of deformation (Deleuze 1992: 5).

The movement towards openness in education is therefore inevitable and inexorable – "openness" to be understood, however, as a new form of "free-floating control" (Deleuze 1992: 4). This is surely an aspect of the logic of Open Learning, then, and the rationale for the emergence of "distance education" as the *modus operandi* for educational practice and development more generally, and more specifically, the notion of "virtual schooling" (Tiffin and Rajasingham 1995). This is the new "immaterial", abstracted form of the postmodern school, or at least that version realised in and though the resources and contexts of digital networks and dispersed spaces. Increasingly schools of all kinds are going "on-line", which means that new forms and relations of presence and absence must be reckoned into the practices of teaching and learning, as well as teacher education, including those associated with notions such as "flexible delivery", from kindergarten through to the university and beyond. This links, increasingly, with new forms of *distributed* schooling – different arrangements and articulations of sites and architectures, times and spaces, bodies and technologies. Boundaries blur and fade – for instance, between "school" and "not-school". Learning becomes "life-long", education "continuing". The school is thus everywhere – and nowhere. This logic is also consistent with, and entirely implicated in, the institutional shift from education, as traditionally understood, to the digital-electronic media as the principal site of socialisation-subjectification – that is, of the production of appropriate social identities.

In summary, then: The changes and challenges outlined here, significantly shaped and organised as they are by emergent forms and intensities of information technology, are to be understood in terms of new ways of "doing education", or of making education happen – of *practising* education. This needs to be seen as taking in matters such as social integration,[17] skills development and training, information access and resourcing, and credentialling – even "childcare". Hence, importantly, a new nexus is to be observed between the principle of information, technocultural change, and the mode of education. This means, in turn, changed and changing forms and functions of schooling, and also new agendas and challenges for teachers, teacher educators, and all those involved in and committed to the idea of the school and the notion of education as a critical-democratic practice.

2

We are now better placed to understand the implications and challenges associated with the notion of "re-tooling", in contemplating the whole question of prospects and scenarios in Australian education. On the one hand, it refers to the emergence of the new information media as a key defining technology in schools and society alike. The shift from print culture and its accompanying "apparatus" to those of digital-electronics means decisive change, on a number of levels. Given the historic role of curriculum as both a *selection* from and a *representation* of Australian culture, it should come as no surprise that this shift also has implications in and for educational practice and the nature and conduct of schooling. Among other things, this means there is a need for (re)new(ed) attention to the educational role and significance of literacies and technologies, their changing and emerging forms, and the relationship between them (Lankshear et al 1996). This has implications for teachers and students alike, and hence for curriculum revision and policy formulation in terms of both teacher education and school education. However, we want to argue that, while entirely and unequivocally necessary, this is still an insufficient condition for understanding and effecting the kinds of changes at issue here. That is to say, the focus shouldn't be on technology *per se*. Rather, as a first-order priority, it needs to be directed to re-

---

17 Understood in terms of social reproduction, cultural transmission and ideological communication.

thinking and reconstructing the larger context of educational and social *purpose* and *meaning*, within which technological development and change is always an integrated element.[18]

The second, less literal sense of the notion of "re-tooling", then, is one of revisioning the school, and of regenerating a sense of possibility with regard to education as a public institution. This means attending to the circumstances of crisis, complexity and change that mark so dramatically the current relationship between schooling and society. As Beare and Slaughter (1993: 16) write:

> If schools are to play a more culturally constructive role than they are doing at present, their work requires some broadly defined social purpose, something that goes beyond purely personal, economic, and short-term considerations which derive solely from what has gone before.

As Beare and Slaughter continue: educators need "a credible vision of a future that works and that reconnects each individual with the wider world", and moreover, "[t]hey need a sustainable, human vision which embodies a set of viable purposes and meanings" (1993: 16). The important point to stress here is the need to bring together vision and strategy, principle and practice, in a single project that combines and integrates critique, possibility *and* programmes for practical renewal and change.

In the first instance, this requires cultivating an attitude of *informed scepticism* with regard to the promises and rhetorics associated with "new technology", with the emphasis to be placed firmly on both sides of this formulation – that is, on being *both* informed and sceptical. In our view, there is no longer any point or value in debating *whether* educators should engage with new technologies; rather, the issue is *how* they do this. Generating a richer, more pluralistic picture of the contemporary scene and its associated debate is an important first step, and elsewhere we have outlined an anatomy of the discursive field associated with educational computing and the relationship between new technologies and educational change (Bigum and Kenway 1998). That account offers different ways of making an educational response to the new information and communication technologies. Taken together, it enables a more

---

18 The following is scathingly indicative of the inadequacy of working in terms of *either* "technology" *or* "society": "Purely social relations are found only in the imaginations of sociologists, among baboons, or possibly, just possibly on nudist beaches; and purely technical relations are found only in the wilder reaches of science fiction" (Wiebe and Law 1992: 290).

pluralistic, comprehensive perspective, one that is not tied to a single view of the world or simplistic assessments of society's capacity to engage or reject the new information and communication technologies.

As we have already suggested, schools have clearly played a significant part in the social acceptance of these technologies. As the world outside schooling continues to technologise and change, however, educators can no longer afford the limited and limiting views which have informed their responses to date. The future of computing and communications media, as with science and technology more generally, will likely remain uncertain for a long period to come. If we are indeed witnessing something akin to the replacement of steam with electric power, then it may be many decades before the impact of the digital revolution becomes clear. It is therefore prudent, surely, to remain open-minded and indeed pluralistic about its long-term implications for schooling. More importantly, we believe that an educationally more principled approach is required, and in this respect we offer a set of principles that we have developed over many years of working with teachers and schools and in our own practice. The principles reflect a broad commitment to social justice in supporting teachers to develop ways of understanding the new information and communication technologies, ways that seek to go beyond the current terms and frames of debate.

Teachers first   This is not simply a claim for more support for teachers in dealing with the new information and communication technologies. Rather, the principle affirms the importance of attending adequately to the personal and professional needs of teachers vis-a-vis computer technologies *before* the needs of students. Importantly, it draws attention to the main reason for neglecting teachers: the view that if students are not properly prepared in the classroom for living in a world with computers, then they will be seriously disadvantaged. While well-intentioned, such assumptions are clearly misguided.

Computers have become more commonplace in the home, and increasing numbers of children now grow up in environments in which they have access to an array of electronic media devices and computers of various types outside school (Green and Bigum 1993; Smith and Curtin 1997). By the time some children reach school, they have considerable skills in using computers and have little or no fear of them. Many teachers, on the other hand, grew up in an environment that had far fewer electronic technologies available and find the adaptation to working with computers more difficult than their students.

Adopting a principle of "teachers first" means supporting teachers to make use of computer and communication technologies to support their personal work *before* using the technology in their classrooms. It encourages teachers to attend to their own needs and interests before that of their students. It is based on the premise that in order to make sound educational choices about using the technology in their classroom, teachers should ideally use it for their own purposes first. The emphasis upon personal use and adoption comes from a broader view that locates technology use in schools as a part of a larger process of social acceptance of computer technology (Franklin 1990), in terms of which the period of the 1980s and 1990s is the early phase of a 30 or 40 year process (King 1996).

As well, what needs to be engaged and better understood here is a widespread "technology refusal" on the part of many teachers (Hodas 1996; Cuban 1986), and indeed educators more generally – something which certainly contains an element of "resistance" but is more commonly and characteristically, we believe, a *generational* feature. That is to say, by and large teachers, parents and the wider (adult) community are all too often caught in a time warp, having been formed and trained in very different technocultural conditions. This is partly a consequence of living on the very cusp of a major paradigm shift – right in its midst, as it were – and here it is both appropriate and salutary to resume the Kuhnian imagery that we introduced previously:

> Because [radical change] demands large-scale paradigm destruction and major shifts in the problems and techniques of normal science, the emergence of new theories is generally preceded by a period of pronounced professional insecurity. As might be expected, this insecurity is generated by the persistent failure of the puzzles of normal science to come out as they should. Failure of existing rules is the prelude to a search for new ones. (Kuhn 1970: 67)

This is surely the situation of many educators today, marked as they are by a "pronounced professional insecurity", facing new challenges and endeavouring to come to terms with fundamental changes in their work and indeed their identities.

Complementarity A principle of complementarity also comes from seeing the educational response to computers by schools as a part of a broader social acceptance of these technologies. In any technology-based transition, some skills become redundant and new skills emerge. For example, for each high technology "tool" that is employed, it is critical to ensure that those skills that complement its use are also taught. A ready example here is the hand-held calculator. In order to use this technology, a student requires at least two complementary skills: the capacity to approximate or estimate an answer, and a knowledge of significant figures. For a "newer" technology such as the Internet, the complementary skills may seem less obvious – although a moment's "teacherly" reflection will bring up such matters as information and research skills, and indeed active orientations to literacy and learning more generally.[19] Even so, some things *are* different. The Internet therefore poses in certain respects unique problems for students and teachers in learning how to find, select and appraise information that, for the most part, has none of the quality assurance methods normally associated with print publications. Since there are as yet few useful precedents for working with information in a space like this, it will understandably take time to identify the necessary complementary skills that a student needs, in order to use the resources of the Internet in an educationally sound manner.

This principle is applicable at other levels of consideration. It is not only in schools that computers and related technologies have made significant inroads. Indeed, it can be argued that the inroads in schools are minimal compared to other locations. The dramatic rise of home computer ownership to support the school education of children makes a consideration of new complementary relationships between school and home absolutely crucial, and a matter of some considerable urgency. It makes little sense for schools to duplicate what is in the home, particularly if the student has better access at home to better technology. Schools might therefore consider offering access to computer resources that is more specialised, such as computer-aided design facilities, music composition facilities, or robotics. An important part of complementarity between home and school is a consideration of those students who have little or limited access to computers. Schooling clearly has a critical role to play here, in ensuring that the least advantaged of the school community receive support, and this may well mean giving privileged access in school time to the "have-nots". In general terms, then, the

---

19 Burbules and Callister (1997) also suggest in this regard the value of certain attitudes or attributes – themselves always *learned* – such as a capacity to live with uncertainty and flux, or to work pro-actively with "excessive" or "incomplete" information.

"complementary" principle encourages a much broader view of the ways that schools construct their responses to the new information and communication technologies.

Access and equity   This is the most difficult but also arguably the most important principle. "Access" and "equity" need to be thought about, and brought, together (Burbules and Callister, 1997). The use of computers in schools always involves choices about resource allocation. The "logic" behind much of this in schools is driven by prior access to information and resources, that is, the technically able and well-equipped are commonly able to make more compelling cases for re-equipping ahead of those who have poor or no resources. We know that in classrooms, as elsewhere, technology tends to amplify advantage. An equity principle acknowledges this, and actively supports an alternative basis for both access to information and the allocation of resources. In addition, however, "access" needs to be re-considered in this context, and to go beyond those positions that see it as simply a technical problem. Rather, as much attention needs to be given to the technocultural *capital* that students (and teachers) bring to the technology when they do have access to it.

As Negroponte (1995: 6) notes, "Computing is not about computers any more. It is about living". In this view, technological competence has become a new "basics" of education, and equality of access and competence must be a key concern for educators. Such competence will eventually have an impact on students' quality of education, as well as their access to jobs (no matter how menial . . .) and retraining, to government information and to learning about critical issues which affect their lives. A consideration of the manner in which all basic needs can be met is therefore absolutely crucial. In addition, as Negroponte implies, as new technologies converge and develop, they will have an ever-increasing impact on our work, leisure, health, lifestyles, national and cultural identities, and social relationships. At the moment, little educational attention is being paid to the manner in which we "produce" and "consume" such technologies or to associated issues of politics and justice. Be it in the workplace, the home or elsewhere, students need to be in a position to assess the costs and benefits of the new communications and information media, and to make wise choices which maximise the economic, social and cultural benefits and minimise the risks and costs. Teaching students about technology, within explicit cultural-critical frameworks, is therefore just as important as teaching them to use it. As one commentator has put it:

> We are not just consumers, we are also citizens. With all this talk about markets and profits in the new digital world-order perhaps it's time to start thinking about what kind of world we want it to be. (Mitch Kapor, quoted in Burstein and Kline 1995: 17)

3

Since the early 1980s, schools have adopted a largely technically-oriented, "heads in" response[20] to the new information and communication technologies. During that time, the transformation of the world outside schools by computers and communication devices with a global range has meant that the narrow basis on which schools have based their responses has become increasingly untenable, and even dangerously so. We argue accordingly that a broader, "heads up" approach is required:

> one that examines the social choices of whether and how to computerize an activity, and the relationships between computerized activity and other parts of our social world. (Kling 1996: 2)

It is only with such an approach that schools can move beyond their current tendency to imagine that if they simply adopt computer use and networking, then they have dealt adequately with the issues associated with now being in a global, "wired" world. This "immunisation" stance is no longer justifiable, especially as Australian schools become deeply implicated in the economic and cultural changes associated with globalisation. Educators must therefore pull their "heads out" of their schools and their investments in schooling and begin to think more holistically, and to consider critically the much broader educational issues associated with the use of computing and communication technologies, in all their profound implications for the new forms and forces of economic and cultural globalisation.

It is clear that schools can make an important contribution here, as they already have historically, in securing the educational legitimacy of the new information media. However, blind faith in technological progress – the Dream of Reason, as we have expressed it elsewhere

---

20 A term coined by Kling (1996) to describe a largely technical "what can this do" approach to understanding and using computing and communication technologies.

(Bigum and Green 1993b) – has not and will not serve schools well, *or* Australian society, and it will continue to limit the ways educators have for thinking about the complex and confusing issues associated with these technologies. The challenge is clear. Schools are well placed to provide leadership in directing the way in which these media develop, not only educationally but more generally, and the opportunity is certainly there to do so.[21] Whether that happens or not will depend very much on the manner in which vision and strategy are brought together in a new educational synthesis that understands not only that schools are always-already "in the futures business" (Beare and Slaughter 1993: 17) but also that education and technology are now thoroughly, inextricably implicated in the renewal of Australian culture.

References

Althusser, L. (1971) "Ideological State Apparatuses: Notes towards an Investigation" in B.R. Cosin (ed) *Education: Structure and Society*. Harmondsworth: Penguin, Open University Press.

Arnold, M. (1996) "The High-tech, Post-Fordist School". *Interchange*, 27(3), 225-250.

Beare, H and R. Slaughter (1993) *Education for the Twenty-first Century*. London: Routledge.

Becker, H.J. (1996) "How Much Will a Truly Empowering Technology-Rich Education Cost?" in R. Kling (ed) *Computerization and Controversy: Value Conflicts and Social Choices*. San Diego: Academic Press, pp 190-196.

Bigum, C. (1995b) "Learning About Limits: Yesterday, Today and Tomorrow as Knowledge Resource" in *Learning Without Limits: Proceedings of the Australian Computers in Education Conference 1995*. Perth: ECAWA, vol 1, pp 161-170.

Bigum, C. (1990) "Computers and the Curriculum: the Australian Experience". *Journal of Curriculum Studies*, 22(1), 63-67.

Bigum, C. and B. Green (1993a). "Changing Classrooms, Computing and Curriculum: Critical Perspectives and Cautionary Notes". *Australian Educational Computing*, 8(1), 6-16.

---

21 As Ulmer (1992: 160) writes with regard to the potential for schools to exercise "significant leadership" in this respect: "The school . . . may have as big an impact on the electronic apparatus as do hardware and software producers, both in terms of what it demands from these producers (what it expects of a mind tool oriented towards learning and creativity) and what we ourselves [that is, educators] contribute to the invention process".

Bigum, C., L. Fitzclarence and B. Green (1994). "Teaching the Lost Generation? Media Culture, (Un)employment and Middle Schooling". *Unicorn*, 20(2), June, 28-35.

Bigum, C. and B. Green (1993b) "Technologizing Literacy; Or, Interrupting the Dream of Reason" in Pam Gilbert and Allan Luke (eds), *Literacy in Contexts*. Sydney: Allen and Unwin.

Bigum, C. and B. Green (1995) *Managing Machines? Educational Administration and Information Technology*. Geelong: Deakin University Press.

Bigum, C. and J. Kenway (1998) "New Information Technologies and the Ambiguous Future of Schooling – Some Possible Scenarios" in A. Hargreaves, A. Leiberman, M. Fullan and D. Hopkins (eds) *International Handbook of Educational Change*. Toronto: OISE.

Bigum, C., L. Fitzclarence, B. Green and J. Kenway (1994) "Connecting Schools to Global Networks One Way or Another" in *Apitite 94*. Brisbane: Apitite 94 Council, pp 359-366.

Bigum, C., S. Bonser, P. Evans, S. Groundwater-Smith, S. Grundy, S. Kemmis, D. McKenzie, D. McKinnon, M. O'Connor, R. Straton and S. Willis (1987) *Coming to Terms with Computers in Schools. Report to the Commonwealth Schools Commission*. Deakin Institute for Studies in Education: Deakin University.

Bijker, W.E. and J. Law (1992) *Shaping Technology/Building Society: Studies in Sociotechnical Change*. Cambridge, Massachusetts: MIT Press.

Bossert, P.J. (1996) "Understanding the Technologies of Our Learning Environments". *Bulletin: The National Association of Secondary School Principals*, 80(582), 11-20.

Brand, S. (1987) *The Media Lab: Inventing the Future at MIT*. New York: Penguin.

Burbules, N.C. and T.A. Callister Jr (1997) "Access to New Technologies: Democratic Challenges", *Critical Forum*, 5 (1 & 2), 32-41.

Burrow, S. (1994) "Macdonald's in the Classroom" in *Schooling What Future? Balancing the Education Agenda*. Geelong: Deakin Centre for Education and Change, Faculty of Education, Deakin University, pp 13-20.

Burstein, D. and D. Kline (1995) *Road Warriors: Dreams and Nightmares Along the Information Highway*. New York: Penguin.

Castells, M. (1991) *The Informational City*. Oxford: Basil Blackwell.

Cooper, R. and J. Law (1995) "Organization: Distal and Proximal Views", *Research in the Sociology of Organizations*, 13, 237-274.

Cuban, L. (1986) *Teachers and Machines: The Classroom Use of Technology Since 1920.* New York: Teachers College Press.

Deleuze, G. (1992) "Postscript on the Societies of Control". *October*, 59, 3-7.

Department of Communications and the Arts (1994) *Creative Nation: Commonwealth Cultural Policy.* Canberra: Department of Communications and the Arts.

Eckersley, R. and K. Jeans (eds) (1995) *Challenge to Change: Australia in 2020.* Melbourne: CSIRO Publications.

Eisenstein, E. (1979) *The Printing Press as an Agent of Change.* Cambridge: Cambridge University Press.

Fitzclarence, L., B. Green and C. Bigum (1995) "Stories In and Out of Class: Knowledge, Identity and Schooling" in R. Smith and P. Wexler (eds), *After Postmodernism: Education, Politics and Identity.* London: Falmer.

Franklin, U. (1990) *The Real World of Technology.* Montreal: CBC Enterprises.

Giddens, A. (1984) *The Constitution of Society.* Cambridge: Polity Press.

Green, B. (1993) "Literacy Studies and Curriculum Theorizing; Or, The Insistence of the Letter" in B. Green (ed) *The Insistence of the Letter: Literacy Studies and Curriculum Theorizing.* London: Falmer.

Green, B. and C. Bigum (1993) "Aliens in the Classroom". *Australian Journal of Education*, 37(2), 119-141.

Hiltz, S. R. (1994) *The Virtual Classroom: Learning without Limits via Computer Networks.* Norwood, NJ: Ablex.

Hinkson, J. (1991) *Postmodernity: State and Education.* Geelong: Deakin University Press.

Hodas, S. (1996) "Technology Refusal and the Organizational Culture of Schools" in R. Kling (ed) *Computerization and Controversy: Value Conflicts and Social Choices.* San Diego, Academic Press.

Iacono, S. and R. Kling (1996) "Computerization Movements and Tales of Technological Utopianism" in *Computerization and Controversy: Value Conflicts and Social Choices.* San Diego: Academic Press.

Idhe, D. (1990) *Technology and the Lifeworld: From Garden to Earth.* Bloomington: Indian University Press.

Illich, I. (1971. *Deschooling Society.* New York: Harper and Row.

Jones, B.O. (1990) "Science, Technology and Futures in Australia". *Futures*, 22(3), 244-252.

Kenway, J. (1995) "Reality Bytes: Education, Markets and the Information Super-highway". *The Educational Researcher*, 22(1), 35-65.

Kenway, J. (1996) "The Information Superhighway and Post-modernity: The Promise and the Price". *Comparative Education*, 32(2), 217-232.

Kenway, J., C. Bigum, L. Fitzclarence, with J. Collier and K. Tragenza (1995) "New Education in New Times". *Journal of Education Policy*, 9(4), 317-333.

King, J.L. (1996) "Where Are the Payoffs from Computerization? Technology, Learning, and Organizational Change" in R. Kling (ed) *Computerization and Controversy: Value Conflicts and Social Choices*. San Diego: Academic Press, 239-260.

Kling, R. (ed) (1996a) *Computerization and Controversy: Value Conflicts and Social Choices*, second edition. San Diego: Academic Press.

Kling, R. (1996b) "Computerization at Work" in R. Kling (ed) *Computerization and Controversy: Value Conflicts and Social Choices*. San Diego: Academic Press.

Kling, R. (1996c) "Heads-Up versus Heads-In Views of Computer Systems" in R. Kling (ed) *Computerization and Controversy: Value Conflicts and Social Choices*. San Diego: Academic Press.

Kress, G. (1995) *Writing the Future: English and the Making of a Culture of Innovation*. National Association for the Teaching of English, Sheffield.

Kuhn, T. (1970) *The Structure of Scientific Revolutions*, second edition, enlarged. Chicago: University of Chicago Press.

Lankshear, C., C. Bigum, C. Durrant, B. Green, W. Morgan, J. Murray, I. Snyder and M. Wild (1996) "Literacy, Technology and Education: A Project Report". *Australian Journal of Language and Literacy*, 19(4), 345-358.

Latour, B. (1986) "Visualization and Cognition: Thinking with Eyes and Hands". *Knowledge and Society: Studies in the Sociology of Culture Past and Present*, 6, 1-40.

Lave, J. and E. Wenger (1991) *Situated Learning: Legitimate Peripheral Participation*. Cambridge, Cambridge University Press.

Law, J. (1994) *Organizing Modernity*. Oxford: Blackwell Publishers.

Lemke, J.L (1994) "The Coming Paradigm Wars in Education: Curriculum vs Information Access" in *Computers, Freedom, and Privacy Conference*, Chicago.

Lowe, I. (1992) "Social Impact Analysis of Information Technologies" in T. Stevenson and J. Lennie (eds) *Australia's Communication Futures*. Brisbane, The Communication Centre, Queensland University of Technology, pp 48-59.

McHoul, A. (1991) "Readings" in Carolyn D. Baker and Allan Luke (eds), *Towards a Critical Sociology of Reading Pedagogy*.

Amsterdam and Philadelphia: John Benjamins Publishing Company, pp 191-210.

Negroponte, N. (1995) *Being Digital*. New York: Knopf.

Papert, S. (1993) *The Children's Machine: Rethinking School in the Age of the Computer*. New York: Basic Books.

Penley, C. and A. Ross (eds) (1991) *Technoculture*. Minneapolis: University of Minnesota Press.

Perelman, L.J. (1992) *School's Out: Hyperlearning: The New Technology, and the End of Education*. New York: William Morrow.

Poster, M. (1995) *The Second Media Age*. Cambridge, UK: Polity Press.

Sassen, S. (1991) *The Global City*. Princeton: Princeton University Press.

Smith, R. and P. Curtin (1997). "Computers and Life Online: Education in a Cyber-World" in I. Snyder (ed) *Taking Literacy into the Electronic Age*. Sydney: Allen and Unwin, pp 211-233.

Stocker, J.W. and R. Eckersley (1995) "Australian Science, Australia's Future: The Role of Science and Technology in Achieving a Preferred Future for Australia" in R. Eckersley and K. Jeans (eds), *Challenge to Change: Australia in 2020*. Melbourne: CSIRO Publications.

Tiffin, J. and L. Rajasingham (1995) *In Search of the Virtual Class: Education in an Information Society*. London: Routledge.

Ulmer, G. (1989) *Teletheory: Grammatology in the Age of Video*. London: Routledge.

Ulmer, G.L. (1992) "Grammatology (in the Stacks) of Hype-rmedia: A Simulation" in Myron C. Tuman (ed) *Literacy Online: The Promise and Perils of Reading and Writing with Computers*. Pittsburgh and London: University of Pittsburgh Press.

6

Doing critical cultural studies
– an antidote to being done to

Robert Hattam, Geoff Shacklock and John Smyth

> For years, I believed that pedagogy was a discipline developed around the
> narrow imperatives of public schooling. And yet, my identity has been
> largely fashioned outside of school. Films, books, journals, videos, and
> music in different and significant ways did more to shape my politics and
> life than did formal education, which always seemed to be about
> somebody else's dreams.
>
> — Henry Giroux, *Disturbing Pleasures*

More than ever before, school life and all that it contains is becoming
marginal to how students inform themselves about their roles as members
of society, understand their social heritage, and permit themselves to
actively influence the quality, fairness and dignity of their life chances.
There are many ways in which young people's identities are constructed
by social, economic and political factors. While school can (and does)
play a part in this, it can no longer expect to be the major place of cultural
learning for young people living at the turn of century (Martin 1996). If
school is to (re)claim an important place in the cultural learning of young
people, its role must shift from one of cultural indoctrination to one of
cultural interpretation, to provide students with informed perspectives
that allow them to critically explore how their society encourages
conformity and limits possibilities for being different in their thinking
and behaviour.

Schools require a space in their teaching programs that is "receptive
of popular culture" (Giroux 1994), within which students and teachers
can develop new ways for studying culture that allow young people to
identify and discuss the whole range of influences which affect how they

97

can think about the way people live together in society. This kind of teaching and learning can refocus classrooms as places that strive to make cultural understanding personally relevant. (Freire and Giroux 1989).

We propose an "Australian cultural studies" that provides a way of looking at the complex nature of daily life and the many varied cultural objects and texts which allow, and prevent, different understandings of the actions of people as individuals and members of Australian society. We see the study of the culture as important for understanding what is, and is not, possible in how identities are made and communicated through messages from the media and other popular (including consumer) images about class, gender, race and sexuality in our everyday lives. Furthermore, we consider that teachers and students studying culture can work at examining specific cultural objects, their influences and effects, in order to make informed interpretations and decisions about the kind of Australian society in which they want to live.

A broad understanding of culture is implicit in the definition of cultural studies proposed here; one in which no particular cultural form is seen as best, strange, or irrelevant. We believe that distinctions between so-called "high", "popular", consumer, and media cultures are arbitrary and irrelevant. All forms of culture shape thoughts about individuals and community and inform our understandings of how we can, and should, behave towards each other individually and collectively. It is our view that cultural studies is a form of "radical contextualism" (Grossberg 1994) which enables a critical examination of social, economic and political practices and the institutions which support and constrain them. It invites a critical view and interpretation of the relationships people form with everyday cultural effects like work, sport, music, school, printed text, television, cinema, art, theatre, consumer goods, advertising, and fashion. It implies a careful demonstration of how those relationships simultaneously construct and disrupt, exploit and enrich, how we view ourselves collectively and individually as Australians. Most of all, a cultural studies would aim to allow a critical stance toward the apparently taken-for-granted nature of highly visible messages about possible ways to live in society. This would involve seeking to understand the history of "common sense" in our society about issues of race, class, gender and sexuality as they are presented in public opinion, science, books, and artwork and through the media and consumer culture. We believe that identifying and naming racist, classist, sexist and homophobic messages in our culture is an essential task of a cultural studies in schools; a task which opens up the politics of being different and its connection to the visions of democratic society as portrayed in cultural texts and objects.

Cultural texts and objects are the obvious forms of popular, media and consumer culture that link young – and indeed all – people as individuals to a common cultural experience and which provide a focus for the thinking and critical discussion central to the work of cultural studies. Cultural objects like music, dance, fashion, television, movies, magazines, advertising, art and new words are influential parts of a society filled with gadgets and various pleasing and disturbing images that affect how individual and group identities are defined, created, changed and disallowed (Aronowitz 1992). These cultural objects have a very real existence because they are consumed by people for entertainment and information in exchange for money. At the same time, they are more than simple possessions because they widely influence how we see ourselves and other people as real human beings. The study of such cultural objects requires students to have access to learning that lets them speak about and be heard speaking about how society's culture influences their thinking on what it means to be women and men, poor and affluent, gay and straight in the places where they live. A cultural studies can provide that place in school learning for "releasing the imagination" (Greene 1995); by putting into words what is, and is not, individually possible as told by the messages from popular, media and consumer culture.

In practical terms, an important part of understanding how we connect with culture in our daily lives can come through looking deeply at our recent exposure to very powerful images (Kellner 1995) about life. Popular figures like Madonna, Michael Jordan and others often become individual style models for thought and behaviour and very influential in and strongly influence how we see our purpose in life. While the specific storylines from media-packaged images of the successful individual that are witnessed, shared and consumed as cultural objects may not last, significant lifestyle metaphors can still powerfully influence thinking, belief and action. For example, through the cultural objects that are her music, books, video and concert performances, movies and "looks", Madonna opens a window on culture in which positions and attitudes about sexuality, gender, race and class are no longer clearly right or wrong (Kellner 1995; hooks 1994). These packaged images flood the consumer market, widely influencing popular taste and fashion as cultural-products of great commercial value, but at the same time they significantly upset taken-for-granted ideas about femininity, sexuality, race, religion, and wealth. They bring those who buy the products into contact, in ways not previously possible, with different and non-conformist ways of thinking and behaving. The significance of Madonna as a cultural object is the window it gives on how individual people can exercise some control over their lives by being different, if that is their choice. In a similar way, the commercial success story of Michael Jordan as "an icon of race-transcending American athletic and moral excellence" (Dyson 1994: 119) contains both positive and negative messages for young people through powerfully influential images about fashion, sport and race. Through cultural studies, students, as "cultural workers" (Giroux 1994), might critically look at and understand the simultaneous possibility for being "cool" and "ripped-off" in spending their money on "being like Mike" (Dyson 1994).

An Australian cultural studies would also look at a range of Australian personalities who make powerful cultural statements as individuals in business, politics, media and entertainment. Many young Australians identify socially with a specific teenage subculture, the so-called tribes (*The Sunday Age*, 12 May 1996), like goths, ferals, punks, homies and grungers, which offer their own important cultural objects that bring powerful lifestyle images. Powerful images of the kind described above can shape and influence attitudes, values and representations of Australians as individuals and community members. We suggest that cultural studies can ask important questions about the power of lifestyle images through taking on critical perspectives about how we see what real people can, and cannot, do in their lives in Australian society.

Media culture, including advertising, cinema and (particularly) television also bring into common view important symbolic images about living together through messages that are communicated powerfully because they are usually imbued with high drama and intense emotion (Kellner 1990). These are different because they are not about individuals, as models, but about the social circumstances, the ways in which people live together in social units like families, gangs, classrooms, and teams. Often these symbolic messages are taken on deeply because of the intensity of their emotional impact and they too, like lifestyle images, influence thinking about relationships and views about race, gender, sexuality and class. Furthermore, television, cinema and video communicate powerful, emotionally charged scenes of supposed everyday life which impact upon attitudes and behaviour about work, urban living, health, family relationships, schooling, masculinity, drug use, and classist lifestyles. By way of example, the contrast between the ways of living portrayed in television shows like "The Single Guy" and "Grace Under Fire", or "The Cosby Show" and "Roseanne" reveal stark contrasts about symbolic visions of individual success, economic prosperity, and family life. Again, students and teachers as cultural workers can discuss the contradictions in how certain racial, class and gendered portrayals of economic and social life are presented as normal while others are not. The ability to challenge symbols about life which remain long after specific storyline details (from an episode of visual entertainment) are forgotten, which convey messages about being socially deficient because you do not live like that – what has been called "cultural homelessness" (Aronowitz 1992) – is the task of a critical cultural studies. A cultural studies would allow students to ask important questions about how some versions of living together have the power to be conveyed symbolically as continuous, normal and just in the imaginary world of television whilst other versions do not appear at all.

We have described how lifestyle images and symbolic messages about how Australians can live together are found in the cultural objects that are met every day in the media, entertainment and consumer goods. In our view, the careful study of cultural objects is necessary to find out about both mainstream and alternate ways of life in Australian society. We propose that these ways of life need to be contested and that students (and teachers) need methods for looking at culture to interrupt the passive and neutral transmission of the cultural messages they receive in a whole range of places – including school. As cultural workers, students and teachers can learn to theorise and politicise their reception of images and symbols about Australian culture to remain attentive to possibility, difference and diversity in the way they live out their lives. In the following sections we outline how an Australian cultural studies would seek this project for the education of young Australians as cultural workers through the development of a critical teaching of culture.

Towards critical teaching of cultural studies

What we aim to outline in broad terms in this section is a way of understanding a critical approach to teaching cultural studies. Our analysis is based on the assumption that schools themselves are important places for the making of cultural understanding. We see importance in teachers and students working together to create critical understanding about culture. Adding to this, we explain how schools can, at the same time, be places that promote cultural learning which both reinforces and challenges the major cultural forms and our understandings of them.

What we clearly need, in an Australian cultural studies appropriate to the complexity of schools nearing the beginning of the 21st century, are forms of teaching and learning committed to what Maxine Greene (1988) described as "reclaiming the public sphere." That is to say, moving beyond a concern with how effective schooling might be used to develop flexible, highly skilled and compliant workers for the clever country, to a more pervasive and profound concern with how schooling might name and oppose the social arrangements that disadvantage the educational lives of so many students. Bob Connell and Viv White (1989) argue this point persuasively, that:

> these inequalities are not a minority problem to do with pockets of poverty in a landscape of affluence. Study after study show a gradient of inequality that stretches right across the class structure . . . There are indeed some findings that suggest the distinctive minority in education are not the poor but the privileged (eg, the gradient of completion rate of socio-economic status becomes sharper towards the top end of the distribution of class advantage, in both national studies . . . (p 108)

We need to focus instead on how success at school might be redefined to incorporate the lives and experiences of currently marginalised and materially excluded groups, so as to confront the distortions to the shape of race, class, and ethnic images which prevent disadvantage being identified with the exercise of power and privilege in everyday life.

We are arguing that schools presently give priority to the stories of the lives enjoyed by well-off, highly educated and socially conforming groups and that, by implication, "a space of inequality and subordination" (Aronowitz 1992: 279) in school curriculum is left for studying other ways of life. At the very heart of the never-ending reproduction of disadvantage within schools is the "competitive academic curriculum" (Connell 1994: 138) and the continuous positioning of some kinds of knowledge as more valuable than other kinds:

> What meanings are considered the most important, what experiences are deemed the most legitimate, and what forms of writing and reading matter are largely determined by those groups who control the economic and cultural apparatuses of a given society. Knowledge has to be viewed in the context of power and consequently the relationships between writers, readers, and texts have to be understood as sites at which different readings, meanings, and forms of cultural production take place. (Giroux 1990: 85)

A useful concept for understanding the way knowledge is selected (or ignored), organised and officially approved as *the* school curriculum is "textual authority" (Giroux 1990). In the competitive academic curriculum, textual authority, or the power used within the classroom to "legitimate both the value of a particular text and the range of interpretations that can be brought to bear in understanding them", (Giroux 1990: 85-6), works to prevent students from seeing their own experiences of life and family circumstances as relevant to their learning at school. Rather than the curriculum being an open space for communication about the world in which we live, the competitive academic curriculum effectively has the opposite effect; it prevents students talking from experience by encouraging teaching and learning practices which focus on "manipulation, sloganising, "depositing", regimentation and prescription" (Freire 1972). Such practices are fundamentally opposed to our view of school learning as an important place for making new understandings of culture in a democratic society. What we believe is being "authorised" as text is an elitist and narrow notion of what counts as text, conceived within strict discipline boundaries that support narrow ideas about what should be the focus of study. To caricature the point a little (representing what we believe to be the reality of many senior secondary classrooms) the dominant authorised textual practice involves the overpowering voice of the teacher drowning out the voices of the students. Success is still being largely determined by an ability to present back to the teacher the right answer. In shedding the traditional subject disciplines – and using a "transdisciplinary" (McLaren 1996) approach – the school curriculum could become an important place for a study of culture in its broadest sense. By "transdisciplinary" we mean not only a willingness to look and interpret differently by drawing on a range of theoretical traditions, but also working to overcome the "borders of militant dogmatism [and] hierarchy-building" (McLaren 1996: 10) that claims there are best ways and superior forms of knowing found only within strict discipline boundaries. A transdisciplinary approach attempts to overcome what Donald Macedo (1993) refers to as the "barbarism of specialization" where investigating the world with abstract, highly specialised, knowledge gives rise to a form of instrumental literacy that is unable to connect what is known with the world as it is lived by real people who struggle and suffer each day of their lives (Macedo: 193).

Now that we have outlined the broad ground that would be covered by a critical approach to understanding culture, we can bring to the discussion some conceptual resources for making critical cultural studies into a teaching and learning practice. We have resisted outlining *the* correct method and instead, within the spirit of the multi-perspectival approach we allude to, we introduce a series of ideas for consideration when making decisions about the content, the cultural objects to be studied, and how such teaching and learning might be practiced in classrooms.

What would be in the curriculum of a transdisciplinary cultural studies?

Michelle Fine's (1991) book *Framing Dropouts: Notes on the Politics of an Urban High School* outlines an important point of departure for deciding what might constitute the content of a transdisciplinary cultural studies in schools. She graphically illustrates how traditional practices in schools and classrooms effectively anaesthetises significant numbers of students in our schools by alienating them from their histories, memories, traditions and trajectories. Such practices also place the onus for failure on the seemingly maladjusted dysfunctional individual rather than on the inability of the school curriculum to chart a successful course for "becoming somebody" (Wexler 1992) for those "most vulnerable in the transition to adulthood" (Freeland 1991: 191). An alternative conception of the curriculum that takes diversity seriously is committed to forms of "entitlement to speak, be heard and respected inside schools" (Fine 1991: 25) such that students themselves are able to "address diversity across the disciplines" (Fine 1991: 219). That is, launching a critical analysis of the structural, institutional and social conditions which privilege "the histories, literatures, sciences, and the arts of historic 'winners' while disparaging the historic 'loser'" (Fine 1991: 218).

We believe this view opens up the school curriculum as a site in which students and teachers make a curriculum around "generative" themes from everyday life, "topical" themes that have local, national or international significance or "academic" themes that lie in traditional disciplines (Shor 1992). Using these three types of themes, we have attempted to typify some possibilities. Clearly some of these topics could easily fit in another category.

Generative	Topical	Academic
hamburgers	peace	multiculturalism
work	Gulf War	population growth
youth	war technology	architecture
Madonna	AIDS	air quality
shopping malls	documentary news	human health and disease
Disneyland	Aboriginal reconciliation	energy shortages
punk	nationalism	nuclear reactors
advertising	television violence	the construction of gender
fashion	globalisation	poverty
cyberspace	guns	information technology
romance	the republican debate	Australian literature
horror videos	unemployment	colonisation

Not only are we arguing for a different thematic structure for deciding the content for a critical cultural studies curriculum, but we also argue for an expanded notion of what objects are to be studied within that structure. For Freire and Macedo (1987) this means "reading the word and the world" in a way that allows students to "check and criticise the history [they] are told against the one [they are living]" (Inglis 1985: 108). Increasing the diversity of the objects being studied to include the "word and the world" is important because of the constitutive relationship between the word and the world. A short quote from Freire and Macedo (1987) helps clarify the nature of this constitutive relationship.

> Reading does not consist merely of decoding the written word or language; rather, it is preceded by and intertwined with knowledge of the world. Language and reality are dynamically interconnected. The understanding attained by critical reading of a text implies perceiving the relationship between text and context. (p 29)

Another way of understanding what we mean by studying the word and the world is to refer to what Norman Fairclough (1992) defines as text. For him text includes both spoken and written language, and visual images and sound effects. Hodge and Kress (1988) argue for also including considerations of layout and visual impact. Analysis of text as defined in this way is often referred to as "social semiotic analysis".

In very pragmatic terms, objects which could operate as texts within a critical cultural studies perspective include the canon (ie, what is traditionally studied in schools), media culture (Kellner 1995) including especially community texts such as junk mail (Luke and Comber et al 1994), material objects from everyday life (Gottdiener 1995), or identities (Christian-Smith 1993; Education for Social Justice Research Group 1994; Ng, Staton, et al 1995).

A suggested cultural artefacts list

The canon	Media culture	Material objects	Identities
text books	magazines	sculpture	living experience
journals	newspapers	visual art	imagination
novels	video and television	everyday commodities	autobiography
encyclopedia	junk mail	shopping malls	
	signs	architecture	
	music	technology: hardware	

Before outlining in broad terms how students might learn a critical cultural studies curriculum, we need to draw attention to some important dimensions of text that we consider aspects of the content. So far we have dealt with the obvious questions: What will be the content? and What objects will we study? To further complicate the story, Fairclough draws our attention to the "multifunctional" nature of texts. Drawing on the work of Halliday, he argues that texts simultaneously work in four ways which he refers to as "identity", "relational", "ideational" and "textual".

> The identity function relates to the ways in which social identities are set up in [text], the relational function to how social relationships between discourse participants are enacted and negotiated, the ideational function to ways in which texts signify the world and its processes, entities and relations ... [and the] "textual" function ... concerns how bits of information are foregrounded or backgrounded, taken as given or presented as new, picked out as a "topic" or "theme", and how a part of a text is linked to preceding and following parts of the text, and to the social situation "outside" the text. (Fairclough 1992: 64-5)

For us Fairclough draws our attention to the complex array of ways that meaning is conveyed through text. If students are to understand this complexity then these aspects of text also need to be considered as content to be integrated into the course and learned explicitly. Students need to be asked questions such as these when reading texts: ˙

- How do you feel about the text?
- What is the text about?
- What view of the world is being represented in this text?
- How is the text trying to position the reader?
- Whose experience is ignored, discounted or misrepresented?

Another way of understanding the complexity of how texts function, and in media culture in particular, is described by Douglas Kellner (1995). Kellner argues for a rigorous investigation of the texts of media culture using a "multi-perspectival" approach and hence the need to "focus on the production, reception and effects of texts of media culture in order to explain the role of the media" (p199):

> a multiperspectival cultural studies ... combines 1) analysis of the production and political economy of texts with 2) textual analysis and interpretation, and 3) analysis of audience reception and use of media culture. (Kellner 1995: 199)

A perspective for Kellner is "a way of seeing, a vantage point or optic to analyse specific phenomena" (Best and Kellner 1991: 213). A compelling argument for a multi-perspectival approach is based on the view that "there exists no one, true, certain, or absolutely valid perspective in which one could" (p 266) make sense of the world.

How could students learn to read culture and imagine better futures?

Setting a direction

Language and images or our cultural objects are constructed and are never innocent. That is one of the best reasons for having an education system. We need systematic and rigorous ways of puncturing, unmasking and getting behind surface appearances. Any education system worth its salt seeks to do that. For example, we need an education that adequately equips us as citizens to do certain things:

- to interrupt and interrogate the images created *for* and *by* ourselves,
- to ask who is doing the representing of our Australian culture, why, and with what motives in mind,

- to engage with those who would construct us through images, idioms, and icons in certain ways, and not in other ways, and

- to debate, contest and re-define how we wish to express the relationships in the various cultural forms and identities we are prepared to accept as constituting a uniquely Australian culture.

- Searching for a distinctive, socially just Australian way of life that is capable of developing cultural diversity (compared to some homogenised and Americanised version) requires that those of us in schools and education continually ask questions such as:

- Why are things the way they are?

- How did they get to be this way?

- What sets of conditions/relationships support the dominant forms of daily life?

- What then is to be done?

These are avowedly political questions, because when we know about and pursue issues of ethics, then we are less likely to be indoctrinated or subordinated by structures and regimes bent on controlling us. In a word, we have agency, we have power, and we are in control.

Obviously, the way in which schools are structured and how lives are lived out within them have important and reverberating messages for what we aspire to, what we value, and what we are prepared to convey to the next generation. If schools wittingly or unwittingly endorse simplistic solutions to complex problems, unjust social relations, and unexamined lives, then there is a fair chance that such unreflective stances will be reproduced in society at large, to our collective detriment.

We can't outline in much detail here what the practice might look like but we do want to outline some important features of a critical teaching practice that attempts to enact the critical sensibility outlined above. A number of educators have developed curriculum frameworks which are broadly critical in orientation and frameworks that would be amenable to a critical cultural studies approach. We will outline three approaches here: "teaching for resistance", "a pedagogy of multiliteracies," and "problem-posing".

In terms of classroom practice, we are advocating what some would describe as the best of progressive practice or a "dialogic method" (Shor 1988) which is summarised as having these features:

Participatory	students should be active in the classroom from the very outset
Critical nature of learning	problem-posing is central to how the content is presented and dealt with in class
Situated	the class text is the language, statements issues and knowledge of the students. From this text the problems are developed.
Dialogic	a return to a desire to talk about and act on the world together.
Desocialising	"to transform passivity into involvement" (p 106)
Democratic	"critical student voices are spoken" (p 107) and asserted
Interdisciplinary	uses material from many areas
Activist oriented	aim is to effect change in society so that it is more just

The Education for Social Justice Research Group (1994) developed a "teaching for resistance" model. The model has three phases: raising consciousness; making contact (with resistance groups in the community); and taking action. This approach was developed in one secondary and one primary school. Teachers were able to reinterpret old themes within a teaching approach that unabashedly aims to develop in students a "sociological imagination". As an example, the topic titles include: *Writing as resistance to racism, Gender and the division of labour, The politics of sugar, racism and land, and Sexism in church language.*

The New London Group (1995) developed a "pedagogy of multi-literacies" with these features: situated practice; overt instruction; critical framing; and transformed practice. This model has evolved from the "genre approach" (Cope and Kalantzis 1993) and the view that reading is a "critical social practice" (Luke and Freebody 1993).

A variation on the pedagogy of Paulo Freire's "problem-posing" approach has been developed by Ira Shor (1987). With this approach the focus for investigation is problematised by considering an ever widening context, starting from the immediate, moving out to national and global contexts, and also considering an historical reading. By this con-textualising of themes from life, students are given the opportunity to understand that no phenomena are natural and that oppressive situations which are the basis of the problems posed are not historically inevitable.

In summary, what we are advocating here could be described as a critical literacy approach to cultural studies. Our conception of a critical cultural studies has the following features: transdisciplinary, multi-perspectival, and dialogic.

Becoming articulate and the struggle for recognition

One of our favourite Michael Leunig (1992) cartoons is called "Being Done To". It represents the seemingly inevitable outcome of life and of being at the mercy of forces beyond our control. "Being Done To" conjures up an image of uncontrollable fate — of our present and future predetermined, with nothing to be done about it, and with our individual and seemingly insignificant lives at the mercy of larger social forces.

For those advocating a critical cultural studies this image of being done to involves being bombarded by the signs of emerging forms of media culture which relentlessly wash through us, and attempt to leave indelible imprints in our consciousness. The power of media culture to manipulate the consciousness of the "masses" has been well documented in some famous cases — such as the Gulf War (Kellner 1995), the so called "peace" in the Middle East (Said 1995) and the case of East Timor (Chomsky 1996). There is also a burgeoning scholarship that is attempting to understand the way in which media culture reinforces alienating gender stereotypes that maintain an ongoing marginalisation of women (Roman and Christian-Smith 1988); and the ongoing complicity of the media in the presentation of racist depictions of the black body (hooks 1992). These new forms of infotainment not only saturate the public sphere — that space in which we struggle to decide what is an appropriate or desirable way to live our lives — but also prevent forms of critical thinking about how we might deal with the significant issues of our age. Anthony Giddens (1994) draws our attention to these: "combating poverty, absolute or relative; redressing the degradation of the environment; contesting arbitrary power; [and] reducing the role of force and violence in social life" (p 246).

Critical cultural studies offers an antidote to this "technological sensorium" (Aronowitz 1992) in which voices and signs circulate as commodities, payed for by those who need to sell their version of the good life. Critical cultural studies offers a method to not only "read the word and the world", but also to open up the possibility of engaging our reading(s) in the practical affairs of everyday life. It is important to stress again at this point the opaque nature of the language or signs circulating in the public sphere or in cyberspace. By opaque, we mean they are not what they seem.

Never has there been a time in which scepticism about media culture is a more necessary requirement of citizenship. In going further in his critique of the American media, Noam Chomsky refers to the media as a "corporate ideological system". Chomsky has been relentless in his critique of the way the American government manipulates the media in order to legitimate foreign and domestic policy objectives. Giroux (1995) summarises this phenomenon:

> The crisis in meaning and politics facing the United States is strikingly evident in the rhetoric of a currently popular group of diverse conservative, public intellectuals who are located and supported financially in the worlds of government, private foundations, and the popular media especially talk radio.

Critical cultural studies not only provides an opportunity to develop a "resistant reading" (Janks and Ivanic 1992) position but also encourages us to practically engage. Critical cultural studies offers more than a theory of the reader – a theory of the critic, of being able to unmask the text as word or the world. Critical cultural studies is also a theory of action – what is practically possible and ethically required as a consequence of the insights of reading.

Critical practice, within a context of concern for a democratic public sphere, involves a struggle to resist the positioning of text in which the possibility of co-authoring is silenced, muted or unavailable. That is, to resist the (naturalised and seeming) inevitability offered by dominating texts masquerading as progress. This involves a struggle towards what McLaren (1996) calls a "democratic imaginary" . . .

> that entails among other things, the following: expanding the vision of a fully social wage; defending the importance of public goods against commodities; challenging the technocratic discourses of the state that reduces citizens to clients and consumers; agitating for the importance of unwaged domestic work and the child raising labour of women; enlarging the view of entitlement; criticizing "the hyperbolic masculinist-capitalist view that individual 'independence' is normal and desirable while 'dependence' is avoidable and deviant" (Fraser 1993: 21); insisting on a view of public provision as a system of social rights; and rejecting the idea of "personal responsibility" and "mutual responsibility" in favour of "social responsibility"; and promoting social solidarity through confronting racism. sexism, homophobia and class exploitation. (pp 8-9)

This is especially difficult for youth in Australian society today. Within the context of the present schooling system and the operations of a youth marketplace that has all but collapsed except for part time work in predominantly service industries, the youth voice has no "enunciative space" (Spivak 1988). In this regard youth are in a similar position to the elderly, the mentally ill, disabled persons, and those in prison. All of these groups are at the mercy of dominating discourses that construct them as deviant (Roman 1996), hence stripping them of a voice of advocacy. Critical cultural studies opens up a space from which youth can speak – and speak from the classroom as a politically sanctioned part of the civil society.

References

Aronowitz, S. (1992) *The Politics of Identity: Class, Culture, Social Movements*. New York and London: Routledge.

Best, S. and D. Kellner (1991) *Postmodern Theory: Critical Interrogations*. New York: Guilford Press.

Calhoun, C. (1995) *Critical Social Theory: Culture, History and the Challenge of Difference*. Oxford, UK: Blackwell.

Chomsky, N. (1996) *Power and Prospects: Reflections on Human Nature and the Social Order*. Sydney: Allen and Unwin.

Christian-Smith, L. (ed) (1993) *Texts of Desire*. London: Falmer

Connell, R. (1994) "Poverty and Education". *Harvard Educational Review*, 64(2), 125-149.

Connell, R. and V. White (1989) "Child poverty and educational actions" in D. Edgar et al (eds) *Child Poverty* Sydney: Allen and Unwin, 104-122.

Cope, B. and M. Kalantzis (1993) *The Powers of Literacy: A Genre Approach to Teaching Writing*. London: Falmer.

Dyson, M. E. (1994) "Be Like Mike? Michael Jordan and the Pedagogy of Desire" in H.A Giroux and P. McLaren (eds) *Between Borders: Pedagogy and the Politics of Cultural Studies*. New York and London: Routledge.

Education for Social Justice Research Group (1994) *Teaching for Resistance*. Adelaide: University of South Australia.

Fairclough, N. (1992) *Discourse and Social Change*. Cambridge: Polity Press, pp 3-4.

Fine, M. (1991) *Framing Dropouts: Notes on the Politics of an Urban Public High School*. New York: State University of New York Press.

Freeland, J. (1991) "Dislocated Transitions: Access and Participation for Disadvantaged Young People" in B. Finn (ed) *Young People's Participation in Post-Compulsory Education and Training*, vol 3, appendix 2. Canberra: AGPS.

Freire, P. (1970) *Cultural Action for Freedom*. Harmondsworth: Penguin.

Freire, P. (1972) *Pedagogy of the Oppressed*. New York: Penguin.

Freire, P. and D. Macedo (1987) *Literacy: Reading the Word and Reading the World*. Massachusetts: Bergin and Garvey.

Friere, P. and H. Giroux (1989) "Pedagogy, Popular Culture, and Public Life: An Introduction", foreword to "Popular Culture: Schooling and Everyday Life" in H.A. Giroux and R.I. Simon (eds) *Popular Culture: Schooling and Everyday Life*. Massachusetts: Bergin and Garvey.

Giddens, A. (1994) *Beyond Left and Right: The Future of Radical Politics*. Cambridge, UK: Polity Press.

Giroux, H. (1990) "Reading Texts, Literacy, and Textual Authority". *Journal of Education*, 172(1), 85-103.

Giroux, H. (1994) "Doing Cultural Studies: Youth and the Challenge of Pedagogy". *Harvard Educational Review*, 64(3), 278-308.

Giroux, H.A. (1994) *Disturbing Pleasures: Learning Popular Culture*. New York and London: Routledge.

Giroux, H. (1995) "Right Wing Pedagogy". *The Cultural Studies Times*. (WWW journal)

Giroux, H.A. and P. McLaren (eds) (1994) *Between Borders: Pedagogy and the Politics of Cultural Studies*. New York and London: Routledge.

Gottdiener, M. (1995) *Postmodern Semiotics: Material Culture and the Forms of Postmodern Life*. Oxford, UK: Blackwell.

Greene, M. (1988) *Dialectic of Freedom*. New York: Teachers College Press.

Greene, M. (1995) *Releasing the Imagination: Essays on Education, the Arts, and Social Change*. San Francisco: Jossey-Bass.

Grossberg, L. (1994) "Bringin' It All Back Home – Pedagogy and Cultural Studies: An Introduction to 'Between Borders: Pedagogy and the Politics of Cultural Studies'" in H.A. Giroux, and P. McLaren (eds) *Between Borders: Pedagogy and the Politics of Cultural Studies*. New York and London: Routledge.

Hobsbawn, E. (1994) "Barbarism: A User's Guide". *New Left Review*, 206, 44-54.

Hodge, R. and G. Kress (1988) *Social Semiotics*. Cambridge, UK: Polity Press.

hooks, b. (1992) *Black Looks: Race and Representation*. Boston, Massachusetts: South End Press.

hooks, b. (1994) *Outlaw Culture: Resisting Representations*. New York and London: Routledge.

Inglis, F. (1985) *The Management of Ignorance*. London: Blackwell.

Janks, H. and R. Ivanic (1992) "Critical Language Awareness and Emancipatory Discourse" in N. Fairclough (ed) *Critical Language Awareness*. London: Longman.

Kellner, D. (1990) *Television and the Crisis of Democracy*. Boulder: Westview Press.

Leunig, M. (1992) *Everyday Devils and Angels*. Ringwood: Penguin.

Luke, A. and P. Freebody (1993) "Teaching Reading as Critical Social Practice" in S. McConnell and A. Treloar (eds) *Professional Development for Adult and Workplace* Literacy Teachers. Canberra: Department of Employment, Education and Training.

Macedo, D. (1993) "Literacy for Stupidification: The Pedagogy of Big Lies", *Harvard Educational Review*, 63(2), 183-206.

McLaren, P. (1994) *Critical Pedagogy and Predatory Culture: Oppositional Politics in a Postmodern Era*. London and New York, Routledge.

Ng, R., P. Staton et al (eds) (1995) *Anti-Racism, Feminism, and Critical Approaches to Education*. Westport: Bergin and Garvey.

Roman, L. (1996) "Spectacle in the Dark: Youth as Transgression, Display and Repression". *Educational Theory*, 46(1), 1-22.

Roman, L., L. Christian-Smith et al (eds) (1988) *Becoming Feminine: The Politics of Popular Culture*. London, Falmer.

Said, E. (1995) *Peace and its Discontents: Gaza-Jericho 1993-1995*. London: Vintage.

Shor, I. (1897) *Critical Teaching and Everyday Life*. Chicago: University of Chicago Press.

Shor, I. (1988) "Working Hands and Critical Minds: A Paulo Friere Model for Job Training". *Journal of Education*, 170(2), 102-121.

Shor, I. (1992) *Empowering Education: Critical Teaching for Social Change*. Chicago: University of Chicago Press.

Spivak, G. (1988) *Can the Subaltern Speak? Marxism and the Interpretation of Culture* in L. Grossberg and C. Nelson (eds) Urbana and Chicago: University of Illinois Press, 271-312.

The Sunday Age (12 May 1996). "What to Wear Out When You Want to Fit In", p 5.

Wexler, P. (1992) *Becoming Somebody: Towards a Social Psychology of the School*. London: Falmer.

7

What to look for in your neighbourhood school

John Smyth, Michael Lawson and Robert Hattam

The various contributions to this book have shone some light on the complex relationship between the type of society we live in (and want) and what happens in schools.

The society being imagined here is characterised as: involving an active democracy which entails the participation of it's citizens in making decisions about the functioning of society (this is much more than voting); citizens that are active, critical, politically literate and possess a well developed sense of civic duty; and recognising the need to ensure a strong voice for indigenous and ethnic minorities in the development of public policy; and, working against the invasion of information technology or technoculture amplifying the existing social inequalities. What this translated to in terms of the school could be labelled the democratic school. An active form of democracy requires democratic schools. Unfortunately, such schools don't come with a neatly packaged checklist of criteria. These are institutions that are borne out of struggle, debate, resistance and contestation – in a sense they have been created despite the current worldwide infatuation with the "conservative offensive" (Centre for Contemporary Cultural Studies 1981) to produce one-size-fits-all schools. The kind of schools we are speaking about are significantly more complex than that.

One way of thinking about the democratic school is in terms of the vision it represents. We would all want our kids to go to a school that has set itself an expansive rather than a narrow or an impoverished set of views. The vision of a school can be expressed in terms of its commitments or values; which is to say, the world view we hold. Commitments can also be understood as framing, or as a place to aim for that might not yet be possible. Commitments are a way of expressing unrealised potential in the present situation – a bringing to fulfilment.

What follows are a set of commitments for the democratic school, and some discussion of what these commitments broadly mean, and what these commitments might look like in a school in your neighbourhood.

We believe that commitments don't make much sense unless they occur within a more widely enacted societal commitment to public education. There is some evidence that such a commitment is on the wane:

> At its root this is a commitment of society. It is society that agrees that it has a responsibility to developing and maintaining a healthy, progressive education system available to all. Governments at federal and state levels must forcefully express this commitment through their actions, not just their words.
>
> Education is an essential right of the citizen. All citizens can demand of the state that education be made available and can expect that such education will be of high quality. If this demand and these expectations are not met then it is the members of the government that can be seen as shirking their responsibilities.

Look for:

- proper resourcing of public schools, in staffing, teaching materials, equipment,
- progressive educational policy that advances the development of all students,
- encouragement of meaningful local involvement in the school.

What follows should be read as a constellation of commitments, in which each set of ideas illuminates the others.

1. Articulating the purposes of schooling

The school has a clear and coherent educational philosophy (Goodman 1992), in which the role of the school in developing society and students is displayed in both policy and practice. There is a strong educational philosophy manifested in the lived experiences of teachers, parents and students. The educational ideology of these places is writ large in all they do, as distinct from residing in policy documents – it is given daily expression in the way people treat one another, and in how they live their educational lives in the school. The school's purposes are clear and enacted in a plan of action to promote learning.

As a parent you should feel that the school will be making good use of the time your child spends in the classroom. You should feel that the school holds high expectations for the growth of your child's capabilities and can articulate these in discussion with you and your child.

Look for:

- coherent explanations of the purpose of schooling
- clear explanations of the purpose of each curriculum area
- expectations that your child will experience success
- evidence of students' achievement in each curriculum area
- evidence of the school's achievements in specific curriculum areas.

---

2. Advancing a concern for social injustice [22]

The pursuit of tolerance is a hallmark of a critical appreciation of difference, and is a distinguishing feature of the democratic school. The demonstration of a capacity to embrace diversity and to debate its features makes a school able to challenge and supplant dogmatic and entrenched viewpoints. The school has effective policies and procedures for including all students and protecting their rights. All students are expected to succeed and the school provides the resources and structures that allow this expectation to be fulfilled across the full range of abilities and activities. This is coupled with the wider view that education and schooling should be a way towards economic independence for all students.

---

22 See Connell 1993.

Look for:

- diversity of viewpoints
- evidence of concern for the least advantaged
- an understanding that disadvantage is not an individual problem
- success accessible to *all* students.

---

3. Continually (re)focus on learning

Schools are not always focused on kids' learning (Hattam, Brown and Smyth 1995). This needs to be the brightest star in our constellation of commitments. All aspects of school life should be interrogated by the question: Does this enhance kids' learning?

Learning should not remain mysterious. Students should be engaged in finding out about their own and other people's lives. This means having frameworks for perception; having ways of analysing information presented to them; knowing how to transform that information and store it in accessible ways; and being able to search for and use that information to solve and resolve other problem situations.

Students in a democratic school will gradually develop an understanding that learning is something that can be individually and collectively regulated, and that there are multiple pathways to completing learning tasks. Reflecting on how learning occurs is crucial in these schools. Teachers in these schools are only one of many sources of learning – who teaches and who has expertise depends upon the particular circumstances. Pedagogical expertise is not fixed – it all depends on the issues and the circumstances.

Another way of thinking about this is to speak about rigour – where rigour is taken to mean the educative relationship between students and teacher. Some people like to talk about educational standards – we think this term only confuses the debate about what goes on in schools and takes the focus away from the nature of the relationship between teachers and students. Schools that take the issue of continually (re)focussing on kids' learning, place rigour squarely on the agenda.

Look for:

- demanding tasks that students can be successful at
- teaching practices that address the question: How does this advance learning?
- genuine attempts to negotiate the curriculum with students
- forms of assessment that are fair but not demeaning
- problem solving and self-managing/regulating approaches to learning
- approaches that involve understanding complexity through investigation
- ways of organising classes that don't rely on flawed forms of streaming students
- evidence that kids are succeeding that go beyond so-called neutral forms of testing.

4. A culture of innovation

There is a manifest sense of excitement about learning activities as shown through the willingness of teachers to innovate and experiment with arrangements for learning, and the activities and products of students in their classroom work (Boomer et al 1992).

The atmosphere in the classroom and the school emphasise possibilities arising from learning, the reward that comes from understanding what the world is like, how it came to be that way, how things work, what could be done differently, and in what ways everyone might share more equitably.

We are not arguing here for mere concern with the avant-garde or the popular. We are pointing to the importance of building on students' desire to comprehend, to understand their world, and to act on it in ways that change it.

So, we expect both teachers and students to be excited about the discoveries they are making, to be showing pride in the outcomes of their investigations, and to be eager to engage this learning in both discussion with parents, and in direct action to change the wider world.

Look for:

- displays of student investigations
- publishing or performance of student work
- teachers talking about their teaching
- teachers explaining their teaching procedures
- teachers undertaking research on their teaching
- evidence of students' social conscience
- curriculum that focuses on and emerges out of the "real" world
- students' projects that "make a difference" to actual lives.

---

5. Enacting democratic forms of practice

Schools should work to open up spaces in which unforced agreements can be negotiated around the school curriculum (Apple and Beane 1995). In particular, the school should be struggling to open spaces for the voices of the most disenfranchised members of the school community.

The school organises spaces for the interaction of *all* of its members; parents can attend school council meetings; parents are invited to engage in discussion with staff; students engage actively in discussion of school policies and practices and carry the outcomes of these discussion to the school decision-making body, where they have representation.

The school also provides spaces and structures for teachers to discuss and develop policy and practice. These structures model the practices they are discussing or using in classrooms. These structures allow for the critical examination of policy and practice, for the expression of different views, and for the working through of issues by the teachers.

The architecture is such that there is space for debate, contestation and discussion as a normal part of the life of the school.

Cooperation is the key organising, curricular and pedagogical concept and there is a strong belief that there is more to be gained through working together than through competing.

Look for:

- who makes the rules
- how resources are allocated
- the structures by which decisions are made
- who has the right to speak
- whether some groups are excluded from a say
- match between what is *said* and what is *done*.

6. Being community-minded

Democratic schools work hard to achieve a shared consciousness of the situated and located nature of the learning process (McLaren 1989). This involves working to be relevant to the community around the school, and being partisan in response to their struggles to live worthwhile lives. It also means breaking the hermetic seal that often contains school life.

The school regards itself not only as being located in the immediate society, but also as having a global perspective from which students see the effects of interaction, and engage in practical and ethical action, at both these levels.

Look for:

- understanding of the global community
- projects that engage local community groups
- issues of importance to the environment.

7. Educative leadership

The commitments to good educational practice that we have listed so far need to be held together, and held onto across time, in an organisational sense. Typically it is the leaders in the school who will work at this holding-on task (Smyth 1991). School leaders are not only those in senior administrative positions: many teachers in effective schools we have studied contribute significantly to the leadership of the school. However, it is also the case that principals and deputy-principals play key roles in these schools. These individuals do not need to be charismatic. They do need to have a clear, strong sense of purpose, and they need to be able to allow others in the school to contribute *their* leadership skills.

Hierarchy, regardless of how it is expressed – status, position, gender, race, ethnicity, class, age – is continually challenged. Hierarchies are regarded as being destructive of educative agenda, and part of the school's educative agenda is to actively confront and contest the forces that construct and sustain hierarchies.

> Look for:
> - distributive decision-making
> - allowing people to make and learn from their mistakes
> - supporting new initiatives
> - joint construction of a view of where the school is headed
> - a continual changing of who is regarded as having expertise
> - constant emphasis on planning and monitoring progress
> - efforts to deconstruct hierarchies of whatever kind.

8. A discourse emphasising critical literacies

This means promoting critical and political literacies not just functional ones that lead to technical literacy (Fairclough (ed) 1992). Schools must be centrally concerned with literacies for active citizenship. Learning to read and write should be based on an understanding that literacy is a social practice and that making meaning requires a "reading of the world and the word". Put another way, reading is about interpretation, how things are constructed, and how they came to be that way. Interpretation cannot be collapsed down to meanings of individual words. Even the simplest narratives require being able to bring a reading of the world to the words.

What gets said in schools determines to a significant extent what happens. This means schools need to sustain a significant debate about the nature of the categories being used to speak about the work of teaching and learning. It also means engaging with the language being used in public spaces – political correctness will be rampant, and so too will being polite to others.

Look for:

- multiple voices and perspectives on issues
- approaches that question the status quo
- seeking out positions that are normally ignored or silenced
- unconventional ways of thinking and acting
- a fearlessness in challenging established ways, just because they are traditional.

Conclusion

As we approach the fresh millennium the maintenance of a viable public sphere is in deep and possibly terminal trouble unless we do something drastic about it. In this book we and our collaborators have argued that schools are central to the reclamation process. We have outlined a constellation of "critical sensibilities" (Soucek 1995) that are necessary benchmarks of any such educative-led restoration of society, based around democratic schooling. While in some respects "the very idea of democratic schools has fallen on hard times" (Beane and Apple 1995), we hope that this book has left three lasting impressions:

- that it is alive and kicking
- that it is possible, and
- that it is worth fighting for.

If you are prepared as Giroux says to "live dangerously" (Giroux 1993) and not be "dewy-eyed romantics" (Apple and Beane (eds) p 103), seeing schools as part of a larger social movement, then the current degradation of public schools might be reversed through a commitment to "finding practical ways to increase meaningful participation of everyone involved in the educational experience, including parents, local residents, and especially students themselves" (Apple and Beane (eds) 1995: 101).

References

Apple, M., and J. Beane (1995) *Democratic Schools*. Alexandria (VA): Association for Supervision and Curriculum Development.

Beane, J., and M. Apple (1995) "The Case for Democratic Schools" in M. Apple and J. Beane (eds) *Democratic Schools*. Alexandra (VA): Association for Supervision and Curriculum Development.

Boomer, G., N. Lester, C. Onore and J. Cook (eds) (1992) *Negotiating the Curriculum: Educating for the 21st Century*. London: Falmer.

Centre for Contemporary Cultural Studies (1981) *Unpopular Education*. London: Hutchinson.

Connell, R. (1993) *Schools and Social Justice*. Sydney: Pluto Press.

Fairclough, N. (ed) (1992) *Critical Language Awareness*. London: Longman.

Giroux, H. (1993) *Living Dangerously: Multiculturalism and the Politics of Difference*. New York: Peter Lang.

Goodman, J. (1992) *Elementary Schooling for Critical Democracy*. Albany: State University of New York Press.

Hattam, R., K. Brown and J. Smyth (1995) *Sustaining a Culture of Debate about Teaching and Learning*. Adelaide: Flinders Institute for the Study of Teaching.

McLaren, P. (1989) *Life in Schools: An Introduction to Critical Pedagogy in the Foundations of Education*. White Plains (NY): Longman.

Smyth, J. (1991) *Teachers as Collaborative Learners: Beyond Dominant Modes of Supervision*. Buckingham: Open University Press.

Soucek, V. (1995) "Public Education and the Post-Fordist Accumulation Regime: A Case Study of Australia". *Interchange*, 26(3), 241-255.

Index

public sphere, 15, 17, 123
purposes of schooling, 3
race, 23, 98, 99
racial vilification, 55
racism, 6, 8, 23, 44, 52, 57
radical contextualism, 98
re-invent and re-imagine schooling, 80
re-schooling, 83
re-technologising the school, 81
re-tooling schooling, 80, 81
re-tooling, 9, 79, 85
reclaiming the public sphere, 102
reculturing the future, 76
releasing the imagination, 99
religion, 99
republic, 27
republican, 29, 30, 40
resistance, 88, 115
resistant reading, 111
restructured schools, 20
restructuring, 21, 43
retention, 16
revisioning the school, 86
rights, 32, 33, 35, 53, 58, 59, 62, 117
rigour, 118
rural, 18
school as a technology, 3
schooling and culture, 3, 4
schooling, 15, 22, 27, 28, 35
schools, 115, 117
selecting and sorting, 2
self-determination, 43
self-managing, 6
self-regulating learners, 12
sexism, 8, 44
sexuality, 98, 99
silences, 8
social and cultural capital, 5
social and cultural formation, 4
social benchmarks, 32, 33
social capital, 5
social cohesion, 35
social conscience, 120
social fabric, 5, 7
social injustice, 65, 117
social justice, 2, 9, 87

social objectives, 60, 63
social solidarity, 32
socially critical benchmarks, 8
socially just, 25
societies of control, 84
socioeconomic backgrounds, 18
sociological imagination, 109
sociology of education, 19
solidarity, 34, 43, 45
space of inequality, 102
spaces of enclosure, 9, 83
special education, 18
streaming, 18
structural inequality, 2
student investigations, 120
student-centred strategies, 39
symbolic messages, 100, 101
teachers first, 88
teachers, 35, 42, 116, 118, 120
teaching for resistance, 108, 109
technocultural capital, 9, 90
technocultural change, 74, 80, 85
technoculture, 74, 115
technologically-textured context, 73
technology as a form of practice, 80
technology refusal, 88
technoscientific culture, 78
technosocial conditions, 74
textual authority, 103
theory of action, 111
tolerance, 38, 43, 44
tracking, 18
transdisciplinary, 103, 110
unemployment, 54, 55
user pays, 10
values, 51
vilification, 58
virtual schooling, 84
vocationalism, 7, 35
voice, 112, 115
wealth, 31, 99
welfare state, 31
wellbeing, 31
White Australia, 64
wired world, 91
young identities, 4, 97
youth unemployment, 7